The Unfathomed Mysteries from
Outside and Within the Universe

TODD AARON

THE
UNANSWERED
WONDERS OF THE
UNIVERSE

Ocean Wave

Ministries

First Edition
First Edition: January 2023
This edition first published in 2023

Illustrations copyright © 2023 by Todd Aaron
Cover photograph copyright © Todd Aaron 2023

Cover Pictures/Canva
Design by Todd Aaron
Cover Astronaut photography by Cottonbro Studio

ISBN 979-8-218-22200-0 (paperback & ebook)

Published by Todd Aaron & Ocean Wave Ministries
www.oceanwaveministries.com
oceanwaveministries@gmail.com

"The world is not looking for more doctrinal proof of the reality of God! It is looking for greater proof of the resurrection or better arguments about creation. The world is looking for Christians who can stand up to every crisis, fear, trouble, and difficulty and remain calm and at rest in the midst of it all. The world needs to see God's children trusting wholly in their Lord."

-David Wilkerson

"A humble person is not one who thinks little of himself, hangs his head, and says "I'm nothing." Rather he is one who depends wholly on the Lord for everything in every circumstance."

-David Wilkerson

"One of these days, some simple soul will pick up the book of God, read it, and believe it."

-Leonard Ravenhill

"If I had spent more time alone with God rather than preaching and planning how I was going to change the world, I would be a very different man."

-Leonard Ravenhill

"The church used to be a lifeboat rescuing the perishing, now she is a cruise ship recruiting the promising."

-Leonard Ravenhill

"He "Yeshua" didn't make the law easier. He didn't make the law harder. He put the spirit behind the law. Because too many people 2000 years ago, and just like they're doing today, are holding onto Jesus and holding onto the world, and hoping they will still get into heaven."

-Rabbi Greg Hershberg

"Any faith that must be supported by the evidence of the senses is not real faith"

-A.W. Tozer

"You can see God from anywhere if your mind is set to love and obey him"

-A.W. Tozer

Contents

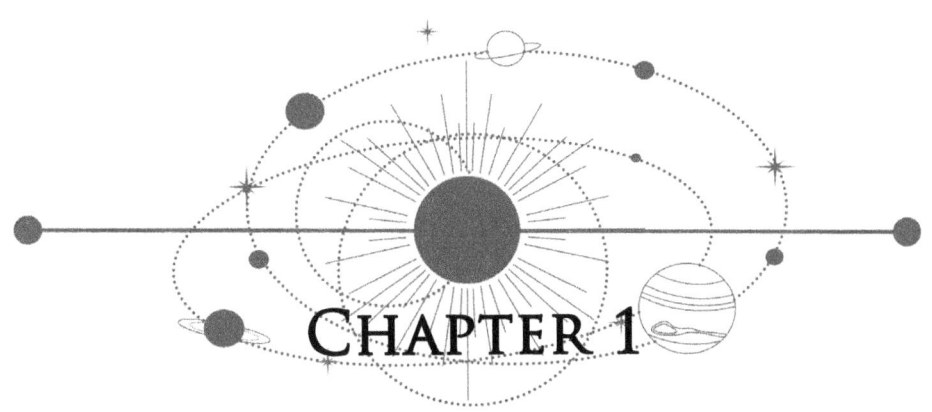

CHAPTER 1

Questioning Life and Reality

The world and universe we are familiar with are full of mysteries, questions, and limitless wonder. It's like an endless book that continues to captivate us. The universe that one can measure and view on a map is estimated to have 2 trillion galaxies. Each galaxy has more, and some galaxies have less. It's estimated to have 400 billion stars like our galaxy, the Milky Way. It takes approximately 100,000 lightyears to pass through our galaxy. How much of that might change within those scientific facts as we explore the depths of our ideas, thoughts, perceptions, and view of life? To what extent has our perception of reality been altered from birth due to our emphasis on money, business, success, materialism, education, and religion? Given that eternity is unfathomable and the size of the universe is incomprehensible, is it possible for someone to truly understand life on Earth?

The questions proceed by wondering, "Who am I? Why do I behave this way? What is the purpose of knowledge? Where did it come from? Where did I learn that? Why do I believe this? Where do my emotions come from? How do I retain my memories? Why do I like this hobby or sport so much? Can money and a job alter my identity? Does everything I do or know matter in the broad spectrum of eternity?" Think about it.

As inhabitants of Earth, we tend to limit our curiosity and exploration to the confines of our minds and the physical boundaries of our planet and its atmosphere rather than venturing into the mysterious unknown beyond the things on Earth that we desire and long for so much. What purpose does it have outside of Earth? Your neighbor, family, co-worker, or friends claim to live freely. They also shape how you, others, and the world should behave. How can you be sure that you don't do the same?

If the world is like a box, who can think outside the vast empty space outside of that box? In that box are billions of tiny pieces of sand, signifying life and people on Earth over its immense years of existence. What has shaped one's entire being while transforming one's mind from each piece of sand that has touched and influenced or been around you? If your thoughts, feelings, emotions, actions, values, character, and attitudes define who you are, how much of that sand around you have formed what's within your heart, soul, and mind? In my search, very few of us have ever been close to exploring outside the box, like that NASA spaceship that landed on the moon. Yet even a spaceship landing on the moon is one piece of sand compared to all the pieces of sand on the tens of thousands of beaches on Earth, just like the galaxies in the universe. While many profess to be free, many claim to know God, and even more believe to be living.

"What is truly living? Who is God? What is being free? Ask yourself, what defines me? Do I know who I am?" If living for eternity is now, the clock never stops. Who created and designed that clock? Here and now, you are living for eternity in an infinite body made up of matter. There is a soul within each human that comprises matter, but the soul interacts with the physical matter of the body. We cannot comprehend or fathom it, but it is put into motion when you move your leg or arm. Everything you do in action, good or evil, interacts with one's eternal soul. The soul is unable to be destroyed nor removed from the universe. Even if a human body becomes pulled into a black hole, the matter turns into dust particles until it vanishes like a body in the grave. The soul persists because it is not composed of matter but instead of something beyond the realm of scientific understanding. The soul connects with your mind, heart, will, imagination, thoughts, dreams, desires, and passions.

The spirit which God gives is the breath of life. It interacts with the holy character of God and his fruitful nature. Love, joy, peace, patience, kindness, generosity, faithfulness, gentleness, self-control, faith, hope, and perseverance come from God's spirit. Before Adam and Eve sinned, God's spirit resided within man even before we had the physical matter of flesh. After sin, which was contrary to the spirit of God, humans were given flesh which then felt pain, suffering, sorrow, death, and the conscience of guilt and shame. All was non-existent before the choice of man with the desire for pleasure and knowledge. The desire to possess knowledge similar to God was considered morbid while indulging in earthly pleasures at the cost of spiritual enlightenment was seen as succumbing to darkness. God wanted to protect all humanity from experiencing suffering, death, sickness, good and evil, and even from the knowledge of eternity. He wanted us to discover contentment with nature, animals, and Him. Contentment is the word Yeshua (Jesus) commands us to find. But in this fast-paced and busy world, many of us have lost sight of the purpose that he has given us.

Instead, many today are using the world's bricks from Babylon to build their tower. The bricks symbolize the world's values, character, morals, ethics, pleasures, and desires. Remember the sand? Are you being used for building that sand castle within the box yet forsaking finding God's design for your life outside the box? God cannot be put in a box, although the world tries to define him in a box like science does with creation and schools do with education. Education and science are without boundaries, yet man tries to limit or redefine what is truth and what is not as if to create a box. The human, which makes a box, reveals how trapped they are and how little they know.

Some brilliant physicists claim there is no God, yet even every scientific equation and theory proves a God exists. The theologian uses the Bible and puts God in a box, yet we observe the Bible as a whole that cannot be contained. The fascinating truth behind the Bible is that God gives just enough to know him, yet never to become too full of knowledge to travel beyond the galaxies in our minds. Many scientists, physicists, astronomers, and religious theologians act like they have figured it out. But all of them continue searching without any end, with unanswered questions for those asking, like defining and comprehending eternity. It's so impossible that the brain has a feeling of exploding at the struggle to fathom and make sense of it all. God even said, "I will destroy the wisdom of the wise." How much more does this prove the truth of God's word and the finite life of a human and their soul?

The influence upon reality distorts our perception, designed and orchestrated by human engineering. The very things that we believe to see, we don't see at all. The world outside our minds that we claim to understand, we are yet to scratch the surface of like the ice in Antarctica or discover all the life in the Mariana Trench. Let alone find the deeply hidden ocean trenches within our minds, or explore what's beneath the ice deep within our hearts. We only glimpse up at the stars if the news tells us about a phenomenon happening above. Do you see what we just revealed? The world influences our actions, thoughts, and will. The motor of society drives us like a Tesla plugged into the electric grid. People gain energy from what goes on around them and form their perceptions and attitudes based on what they are told or hear from outside sources. One often believes it's their thinking and that they are smart enough to navigate the roads in life without plugging into the system. Yet they often fail to realize that their charge and energy come from the world or the box they created.

Indeed few hardly explore the Bible like the universe because they are too busy looking at it with a telescope and a highlighter. In comparison, even fewer are willing to explore their heart, soul, and mind. Many are too busy allowing the world around them to program them like a computer program. At the same time, people are too busy searching for quick answers in the world, like typing in ChatGPT. They forsake the archaeological discovery of one's inner self and independent freedom God designed for their life. The sad reality is that man has a blueprint for society between business, religions, schools, colleges, social media, and news running the engine of Babylon. They cannot break free from the prison within themselves. The box of the world is the prison of humankind. Every human and living thing has a 100% chance of death, yet few want to think about eternity now, let alone what goes on outside the world around them. The universe constantly expands as we speak, and every second the Earth travels around the sun at 67,000 mph or 18.5 miles per second. If one is outside America, that's 107,807 km/h or 29.7 kilometers per second. Yet we don't even feel the motion nor give any thought that we are always moving. How many consider how the universe is expanding at 163,000 mph, or 262,278 km/h? What about that every second that goes by is another second closer to the day your heart stops? Is how you're living now truly worth eternity?

If God gives the soul and the breath of life is his spirit within, how can one be sure that their life here prospers with a God-given purpose?

The world and everything within it is moving quickly, and it never has time to slow down. But the question remains, are you slowing down within to be still with God? In ancient Japanese culture that still exists in some communities, they slowly plant many crops. Within this culture, they see it as a way of life that activates the five senses and brings oneself peace from the outside world. They also believe it's not just about eating but also part of helping others while connecting to God. In America, it's often about eating, social media influences, religious or off-grid influences, or a woman taking pictures of their cucumbers to boast about their hidden internal desires. Who is like those who delight in growing crops without showing the outside world? Who can delight in living up to their morals and values without having outside influence? Who can be satisfied and content with the five senses God has given us, and who is within? Many people never genuinely feel contentment, but it is a state experienced by objects such as galaxies, nebulas, and stars in the immense universe. Total peace and contentment without worldly wants.

Do we know what exists on Earth or beyond the galaxy? Imagine a place without ever knowing life without contentment. A life where wants and desires are absent, and the influences of outside forces have no impact on how we think, act, and live. Jesus says the rocks would cry out in praise if people were silent! Imagine that! According to the book of Romans, the entire creation suffers from sin and eagerly waits for deliverance. It's hard to fathom Earth's commotion, business, and chaos. Around the world, we hear planes, trains, cars, trucks, motorcycles, horns, shopping, buying, news, music, etc. We are never having rest and never truly finding peace. Even we, as humans, try to escape the world around us with vacations and retreats. We still long for more within without finding that solemn rest or contentment in this world.

In Revelation 18:5, we read about how sin has piled up to the heavens. How can this occur? Think about this for a moment, if you throw a ball or water bottle up in the air and it takes three seconds to hit the ground, the Earth has traveled 55.5 miles or 89.1 km in the Milky Way. If you tell a plant negative and hateful things, that plant will die. But if you tell it positive and kind things, that plant will thrive and grow. Likewise, every act of force or movement puts energy into the universe. If sin is a negative energy, how will that affect the Earth? Can it cause earthquakes, tornadoes, volcanic eruptions, tsunamis, flooding, etc? How much more will that affect the universe? Asteroids, comets, solar flares, and eclipses are not merely natural anomalies. It's the effects of negative energy released from Earth and affecting the ecosystem of the universe.

Genesis says God gave us the stars and planets for signs and seasons. How do you think the astronomers and astrologers knew when Jesus was born when he came into this world? They knew by the signs in the stars! We have signs and wonders today, yet some ignore them unless the news tells them to look. While others worship and praise it as if they were gods and give wisdom to our future and inner being through zodiacs and horoscopes. Remember I said how Solomon mentions nothing new occurs under the sun? These ancient influences within the box shape and mold our being, from our souls to the depths of our minds.

The Bible tells us that the universe "will pass away with a great noise, and the elements will melt with fervent heat." How can this be? Gravity, electromagnetism, and thermodynamics all existed before man sinned, yet without all three, how could the above verse hold as valid? God had in mind how to deal with the universe in the case of sin. Sin existed from the falling of one-third of the angels before the creation of man. Think about it: before man's fall and sin, we didn't know what work, sweat, giving birth, or suffering was. There was no knowledge of darkness, comprehension of the universe, or guilt and shame. No questions about the unknown existed, except man wanted to become like God.

These inner desires came about after man's sin, and as a result, seasons and mysteries of the universe occurred, and eternity baffled the inner mind. Humans understood the toil and labor of this life and the depths and heights with wonder about the universe above. Before, God walked with humans in the garden as Adam and Eve heard his footsteps and voice. Afterward, God could not be found in physical terms because the man God banished from the "perfect and good" place called Eden. As a result, God had a plan for humanity, in which the seed that God placed inside of man was evil and corrupted. As the proof on Earth becomes revealed, we begin to see the metabolic process of plants and animals, the expansion of the universe, and solar and stellar burning. We started to see stars die, animals die, animals eat each other, and plants and humans withering, killing each other, and dying. This design was not God's ultimate plan, yet it was in his plan to redeem and save humanity because of his love for us.

An example of this is Babylon. It was raised to the sky by human design. Its purpose was to unite all religions, beliefs, desires, and passions into a single entity. Each wanted to make a name for themselves and defy the God of creation for the creation of human design. This plan ended with confused languages and multiculturalism, which the United Nations and European Union effortlessly aim to raise and restore. God again tried to save humanity through a global flood, proven by coral on top of Mount Everest, dinosaurs dead on every continent, and archaeological proof of the exact biblical dimensions and wood of Noah's Ark discovered in Turkey.

The scientific idea of Pangaea and Mount Everest once underwater sounds like a boxed ideology to push God out and give credence to man. Similar to the notion of HAARP and the government controlling the weather with an agenda to push global warming. Once again, like Babylon, they credit man, not God, who holds the entire universe. Yet God is incredibly patient with us all, desiring none to perish but for all to come to repentance so that they might have eternal life.

Global warming results from negative energy and sin. If the Earth is heating up, it confirms what was written 2,000 years ago in the Bible in Revelation. The sun was so hot that it scorched the people, and they cursed God rather than repented to God. People prove that God exists by the very words they speak when it's hot outside by saying, "Oh my God, it's hot" or "Jesus Christ, it's hot out here." Why don't they say, "Oh my Buddha," Or "Oh my Muhammad." Or why not "Oh my Vishnu and Shiva?" Because deep down inside, a man wants to follow what they desire, designed after man, rather than the law of creation that God set forth before man existed. Yet they instinctively know that a true God has power over these boxed religious ideologies.

You might ask the question, why would God create man if he knew that they would sin? It's an easy question to think outside the box. God already created the angels, yet he was unsatisfied with angelic beings; a third of them sinned. He said in Genesis, "Should we create and make man into our image?" It was an open question. Who was he speaking to? I find it fascinating that science now gives credit to a man who discovered the "god gene," which proves that there were two in the beginning.

The word is also sound and light, which both claimed to create the universe. This discovery then baffles scientists on how both met and came into being, and others give up and say, "The universe could have just existed." Yeshua said he is the word and the light that became flesh. He revealed this in his life by living without sin, doing what was good, healing the sick, giving sight to the blind, raising the dead, and calming the storms and weather. He was proving the restoration of Eden to all who believe and live by faith before the kingdom comes. He came to demonstrate his authority over sin, the cause of death, and the entire universe. Even the stars were aligned and obedient to him from birth, bowing down in worship to the God of creation. How could a man perform such miracles if he did not have power over light, darkness, energy, and sound? The fact is that he did. There were tens of thousands who saw and witnessed it. It is your responsibility to personally witness the miracle and experience the unchanging power of God's saving grace. It has not been withdrawn and is available to all.

He says, "Draw near to me, and I will draw near to you." Again he says, "Cleanse your hands, you sinners, and purify your hearts, you double-minded." The double-minded have one hand in the world, while the other lives for God. One cannot be in a relationship with a man or woman hugging them with one hand while holding hands with someone else. God is jealous and desires our faithful devotion, loyalty, and love for his ways. He will not force you to remain in a relationship with him, but one will miss out on true love if one chooses not to commit their life to Jesus the Messiah.

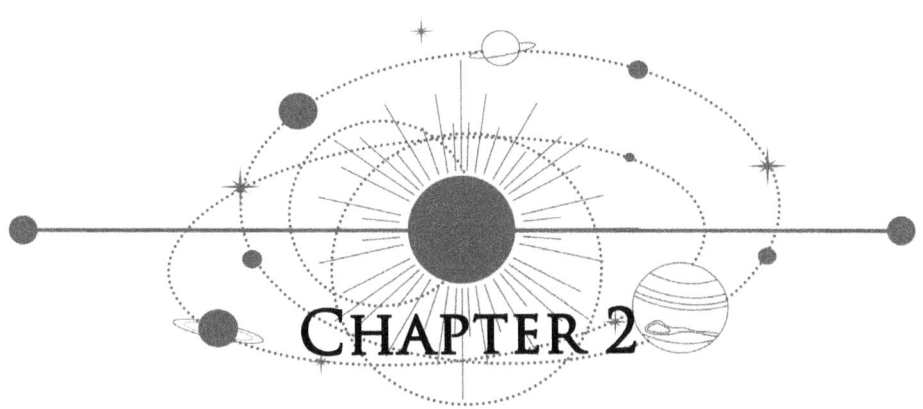

CHAPTER 2

Faith and the Universe

aith is a word that scientists often hate hearing because they want physical proof of what they believe is real. Think about the box again and what is inside that shapes our reality and perceptions. It takes faith to trust in a plane's pilot, the engineers, and the mechanics that put the plane together to get you to the next destination safely. It even takes faith to believe that your heart will beat a minute from now and that you won't die from heart failure.

Science and the world continually want evidence, yet even science constantly changes and evolves from one year to the next. It changes like the seasons, and discoveries are evolving as society and clothing styles evolve every decade. Whether people know it or not, they are changing, just like science—some for the better and some for the worse. Nevertheless, we are all changing, whether our clothes, body composition, hobbies, desires, values, or even jobs. Some of us make errors, and some of us have successes. We don't need evidence of the changes that often occur around us or in us to prove the actions of change reveal themselves as true.

Science is the same way, it's constantly changing and evolving, yet some have errors, and some have truths. The remaining portion remains a mystery and neverending wonder.

The world as a whole is similar to the box I spoke of earlier. It's as if someone has a puzzle in front of them on a table, observing the picture outside the box. They see the sight of the puzzle before them, but they use human methods to put it together to make the image they see with their eyes. But who has the puzzle inside their mind, not put together by human design, hands, or methods? Who can see the puzzle image without their eyes yet still believe that the puzzle maker exists? The puzzle that people put together on the table was created somewhere and by someone. Likewise, is the puzzle created by others or God in your mind? What has shaped one's image of reality? What shapes or designs are from the world or not from this world? Were the puzzle pieces from someone who cut and molded them to make one's own designed image? Is one creating their design and puzzle from within? Or is God cutting the shapes and helping you put the puzzle together?

God is the same yesterday, today, and forever; he does not change. Yet humans and our thoughts, actions, and desires change over time. As Solomon says, "There is nothing new under the sun." There is much wisdom in those words. What has already occurred in the world will be done again, and what has happened today has already occurred in the past. Every action and deed someone takes, whether good or evil, has already happened. Take the sandwich as an example. It's been around since ancient and historical times. But the shape, texture, types of sandwiches, and appeal behind them changes over time. Nevertheless, the sandwich is still a sandwich, whether pastrami, peanut butter and jelly, or turkey.

Humans are the same way. Cultures, religions, diets, traditions, and ways of living evolve. Humans tend to hold on to some form of ancient lifestyle or influence. People pick and choose religions and cultures that fit their values and desired lifestyles—frequently conforming to the traits and characteristics of those beliefs and lifestyles around them. But how many conform to the image of God?

God tells us not to create a graven image of him, but why does he say this? God doesn't want us worshipping something created by human hands and design. God wants us to worship Him in Spirit and truth. Yeshua tells the Samaritan woman that a time is coming when they will no longer worship on Mount Gerizim or in Jerusalem but in Spirit and truth. The Spirit will cause us to walk in his characteristics, morals, and values. The truth from above, planted within us, will testify to what is right and wrong. Deuteronomy 30:14 and Romans 10:8 say, "The word is near you; it is in your mouth and heart." It's close to us so that we might obey it by faith. As Hebrews 10:16 and Jeremiah 31:31-34 says, "This is the covenant I will make with them after that time, says the Lord. I will put my laws in their hearts and write them on their minds." The covenant is open to all who repent and believe.

Believing is a lifestyle of choosing to dedicate your life to Jesus and walking in the path of his ways. Don't worry whether you will do it perfectly. As he says in John 15:26, "I will send you a helper from the Father; the helper is the Holy Spirit of truth who comes from the Father. When he comes, he will tell you about me." How wonderful it is that we can receive a living spirit within us that nothing can take away from us. It convicts us, bears witness to us, raises guilt in times of error, teaches us how to live holy, and say no to sin. The Spirit is true. It teaches us the ways of Yeshua, God's kingdom, and the Word that became flesh.

I reflect upon the times before I came to know Yeshua. I went through the motions of religion. I memorized the Torah portions and verses within the Word. The amount that I remembered shocked the leaders of the congregation I attended. Nobody had ever done it before, nor had they ever heard of it. I thought I had faith and knew God, but little did I know how far away I was from God. Sure, did God allow me to memorize and comprehend written text with a gift from above? Maybe. But he also allowed me to run into a tree so hard that I forgot everything I ever memorized during my younger years. I had only forgotten the religious texts, parashah, and verses. However, I have a clear memory of everything else in life.

It's fascinating because when I hit my head, I saw a man standing in a white robe pointing at me in the darkness around me. I blacked out and encountered head trauma while bleeding on the ground. Who was this man? Why did I only forget what I learned in religious schooling right afterward, shocking the minds of so many? Could it be that God was saying, "Forget what man has taught you, designed for you, and molded within you; when you truly find my son, I will teach you." I didn't know it right away, but after, I couldn't memorize religious texts or scripture any longer. How could this be? It wasn't until I learned to know Yeshua that I was undoubtedly set free! I began to understand everything, old and new, and my memorization returned. Yet this time, I saw the Word differently.

When someone tells me that Jesus is not real, tries to change my mind to believe their religion, or tells me that the new covenant hasn't occurred yet, I can't prove it according to science, but God delivered me from sin. I felt a heavy burden lift from my inner being, and the Holy Spirit enter my body! I felt such joy and peace, yet sorrow, tears, and laughter. I suddenly had power from my inner soul, not only to obey

God's Word but a pure desire to obey it! I had the power to forgive and love. It was not just the human effort of humanitarianism or religious works. No! It was a sincere heart, soul, and mind change with a love I've never experienced! I knew how to pray and understood the Word clearly. Everything I read burst forth a new life I had never experienced before. I felt His laws within my heart and mind. My thoughts wanted to obey and live for Him! My heart desired and understood his ways! I knew I had to tell the world about this new epic discovery! Why would I need the world to define what they believe is real when God has given me such a gift and unfathomable experience?

I don't need to search for anything else under the sun or in the universe, for I know the living God for myself, with such confidence and assurance. Man cannot sway me to believe in their God in a box of ideologies. Why do I need to travel 13 billion light-years if I have already found it in the universe? Why would I believe in something contrary to what I have discovered if I have yet to search empty-handedly for the very thing they are trying to convince me to believe?

Let's reflect upon the thought of the universe for a moment. Each of our bodies contains periodic scientific elements. 99% of the human body comprises six elements: hydrogen, oxygen, carbon, nitrogen, calcium, and phosphorus. The remaining percentage includes the remaining mass: sodium, chlorine, sulfur, magnesium, potassium, and other minuscule trace elements. We also are made up of matter in the form of proteins, fats, DNA, and carbohydrates. Scientists discovered fifty-nine elements in the Earth's crust are in the human body. Proving Genesis 2:7, "The Lord God formed man of the dust of the ground and breathed into his nostrils the breath of life, and man became a living being." How amazing is the creator of the universe? He is so great that his fingerprint is a type of spiral. Human fingerprints, DNA, cells, flowers, sea shells, galaxies, etc., all exhibit this spiral pattern. Despite each of these entities having a distinct design, a close examination of the human eye reveals a striking resemblance to a galaxy or nebula. God says the eye is the gate to the soul while also proclaiming that he is the gate. How many have looked beyond the eye or thought beyond the galaxies? How many have discovered the gate of God's kingdom? Who has created each human alive with a unique and original design? God designed you to be special, unique, and one of a kind. Don't believe me? Look at your fingerprint. Look beyond what you can't see, like your DNA. It's one of a kind, unlike anyone else's alive or anyone who has ever lived since human existence. God had a plan for you with a custom design within your body and soul.

If, on average, there are 80 to 300 million sperm cells that get released into the uterus of a female, isn't it amazing that you were the fastest to the egg? In modern Western times, great multitudes claim that a baby has no soul in the womb. If this was true, why would John the Baptist in Luke 1:15 receive the Spirit in the womb? Why would God say in Jeremiah 1:5, "Before I formed you in the womb I knew you, before you were born I set you apart." God plans for all humans to be set apart and receive his Holy Spirit even from the womb. Consider this: why would you have a unique fingerprint and tongue print, unlike any other human, if God didn't plan for you to live set apart with your unique gifts, talents, purpose, and soul? How can I find that purpose and plan?

Yeshua says in Matthew 23:13, "Whoever exalts himself will be humbled, and he who humbles himself will be exalted." Think about the life of Moses; was he any different than you and I? He might have had a long beard and more hair hanging off his head. But let's look back at his life and maybe why God used him and chose him.

Moses was disgusted and distraught by the lifestyle of Egypt and took no pleasure in it. Hebrews 11:25 says, "He chose to be mistreated along with the people of God rather than to enjoy the fleeting pleasures of sin." He fled from being called a child of Pharaoh and having power, riches, luxuries, and pleasures. How many in the Western-influenced civilization could fathom that? If you're a child of the president, how many would want to live in a tent in the desert for 40 years? Moses fled with nothing to carry except the clothes on his back, refusing to look behind him. Later, God called him back to deliver and rescue the people from Egypt. You can imagine that during those 40 years, he had ample time to think, look inside, empty out himself, and pray.

God knows the intentions of human beings' hearts, souls, and thoughts. Psalm 53:2 says, "God looks down from heaven upon the children of men, To see if there are any who understand, who seek God." Numbers 12:7 says that Moses was faithful in all God's house and that God speaks to him mouth to mouth. Why would God reveal himself to Moses in a burning bush, give him his laws, and reveal his Spirit formed in a cloud? God revealed himself inside his heart, mind, and soul. God says in Deuteronomy 6:4-7 and Matthew 22:37-40 one must love him with all of their heart, soul, and mind. That's their entire being, inner being, desires, will, purpose, and longings.

The revealing of the Spirit and fire is nothing old testament. We see it in Matthew 3:11, "He will baptize you with the Holy Spirit and fire." Not only did Moses experience it, but each person alive could experience the Holy Spirit and fire! Each person living now has the opportunity for God to speak to them mouth to mouth. Unfortunately, the busy lifestyles, the hustle and bustle, chaos, and entertainment consume our inner being. Many people do not pay any mind to the longings of the inner soul but instead replace it with the fingerprint and DNA of the world.

When you look into your eyes, what do you see? The pupil of the eye appears filled with blackness, great mysteries, and wondrous depths. The center of the eye is like a black hole within the universe of one's body to the soul. The black holes in the universe suck in and swallow up whole stars. Likewise, the eye can pull in "stars" from the darkness into our souls. Your eyes may see the stars, known as celebrities, and idolize them, whether on TV, music, radio, or billboards. They may suck in video games, social media, news, sports players, and other people's personalities and influences. Whatever the eyes see has the potential to pull in outside mass within our souls. What you see can change and re-program God's design for one's life since the womb. Abortion is not the greatest threat to a fetus-the greatest threat is when the child is born. The world's influence can corrupt the soul and destroy the heart and mind of a living soul.

God tells us not to worry about what we will eat, what we will drink, or what we will wear. He explains that the pagans, those who don't know God, worry about these things. Yeshua says to serve Him and His kingdom first, and then God will add those things unto you when we focus on Him. How many deceive themselves into thinking they follow God's teachings yet prioritize things that cause stress and anxiety over God and His kingdom? How many people fall into this trap within the vast universe of their souls?

Do you see now how the eyes are the gateway to the soul? The soul can be influenced by what we perceive, see and desire as pleasing and appealing. As 1 John 2:16 says, "For all that is in the world the lust of the flesh, the lust of the eyes, and the pride of life is not of the Father but is of the world." Since we know about the lust of the flesh and desires of the eyes, how can we be sure that we don't have the pride of life?

Let's go back to the story of Moses. Do you think he had any pride in the life of Egypt? What about the lust for what was within it? The answer to this profound internal question is a firm no! After all, he left Egypt for 40 years, went back to rescue the Israelites with God's help, then spent another 40 years in another desert wilderness until his death. That's truly a life to admire, as we see love for God and people. We know Moses loved people tremendously despite how many modern religions portray him. In Exodus 32:10, when God was angry at the people for committing adultery, they built the golden calf while Moses was on top of Sinai for 40 days and 40 nights. God then provokes the thought to Moses and says, "Now leave me alone so that my anger may burn against them, and I may destroy them. Then I will make you into a great nation."

Do you see how God tested Moses? How many today look out in the world, and deep within their heart, they desire to destroy it all? Imagine for a moment if God told you this. How would you react? Look how Moses responded to God in Exodus 32:11-12 "Then Moses pleaded with the Lord his God, and said, "Lord, why does Your anger burn against your people whom you have brought out from the land of Egypt with great power and with a mighty hand?" Why should the Egyptians say, 'It was with evil intent that he brought them out, to kill them in the mountains and to wipe them off the face of the earth'? Turn from your fierce anger; relent and do not bring disaster on your people."

Wow! Do you see the heart of God within Moses? He was concerned about the people and how people would perceive God! How many today are concerned about the lives of others and also the perception of God that one may see within you? How many are praying for others while being set apart so that others might see the image of God within them? I don't know about you, but I see the light of Christ within Moses. Deuteronomy 18:15-19 and Acts 3:22 says that a prophet like Moses would arise and do all that he says. Yeshua himself says, "If you believed Moses, you would believe me, for he wrote about me." The same voice speaking to Moses on Mount Sinai is Yeshua speaking. The voice that trembled and thundered so loudly at Sinai was Yeshua speaking, which brought great fear to the people. As Hebrews 12:18-20 reiterates, "For you have not come to a mountain that can be touched and to a blazing fire, and to darkness and gloom and whirlwind, and to the blast of a trumpet and the sound of words, which *sound was such that* those who heard begged that no further word be spoken to them. For they could not cope with the command, "If even an animal touches the mountain, it shall be stoned." Even verse 21 says that Moses trembled with fear. As we read on, we realize that because of the sacrifice of Yeshua, we have come to accept the new covenant. We are washed in the blood of Jesus and cleansed to draw near to him.

Hebrews 12:27-28 says he will shake the heavens and the Earth again. Everything that's living and things created will be shaken so that the things that can't shake are what remain, which is his holy Spirit. As it's written, those with a firm foundation without being shaken "serve God well pleasingly, with fear and reverence." They are those, as it's written in Philippians 2:12, who work out their salvation with fear and trembling.

In Matthew 6:22, we are not to look at the speck in our brother's eye while we have a log. If that is how we live, we cease to work out our salvation with fear and trembling. Everyone at Mount Sinai trembled and shook with fear, and everyone at Yeshua's crucifixion trembled with fear after he said, "It is finished." The ground shook and quaked with power, and the clouds grew dark like Sinai. How much more should one revere and fear the Word of God when he says, "Do not judge" and "Love your neighbor as yourself." How much more should one have a heart like David, who said in Psalms 119:18, "Open my eyes, that I may behold wonderful things from Your law." Jesus even repeats this desire in others in Matthew 13:16 "Blessed are your eyes, because they see; and your ears, because they hear." Are you beginning to see the importance of desiring God's ways over the world's? Are you starting to see how small humans are significantly used for God's purpose and plan?

Let's look at the life of Elisha when his servant became fearful of the armies surrounding where they were staying. Elisha says in 2 Kings 17, "Elisha prayed and said, "O Lord, I pray, open his eyes that he may see." And the Lord opened the servant's eyes, and he saw; and behold, the mountain was full of horses and chariots of fire all around Elisha" In the same context, many have heard the song "Open the eyes of my heart Lord," yet we cry out in the same prayer. "GOD, OPEN THE EYES OF

MY HEART SO THAT I MIGHT SEE THE WONDEROUS THINGS IN YOUR LAW, THAT I MIGHT NOT LIVE IN FEAR, THAT I MIGHT SEE THE ETERNAL PLAN RATHER THAN THE TEMPORARY!" God opened the eyes of Elisha's servant, and he saw the mighty power of God with all of his angels in the glory and majesty of God. Our desires, purpose, and will should be aligned with eternity in mind, not setting our hopes and eyes upon things on Earth. Paul says it best in 2 Corinthians 4:18, "while we look not at the things which are seen, but at the things which are not seen; for the things which are seen are temporary, but the things which are not seen are eternal."

The danger of taking your eyes off eternity has severe consequences. It can give way to the lust of the eyes, desires of the flesh, and the pride of life. David knew this very well when he fell short by taking pride in power and numbers. As we read in 1 Chronicles 21:16, "David looked up and saw the angel of the Lord standing between Heaven and Earth, with a drawn sword in his hand extended over Jerusalem. Then David and the elders, clothed in sackcloth, fell facedown." David took his eyes off eternity and failed to see eternity. But when 70,000 people died from pestilence, it gave a blow to David's rising earthly pride. When that outcome shook David, he redirected his eyes to Heaven rather than Earth. God opened his eyes to see the angel about to strike Jerusalem. Upon seeing it, David and those with him repented, and God had mercy on everyone. You see, one man's pride can devastate many people. When one loses faith, it can cause eternity to drift away. When you gaze and focus into the depths of the heavenly realm, your eyes will catch a glimpse of the glory of God. One who loses sight and becomes consumed with Earth's problems can be darkened with the blindness of black matter sucked within. The world can consume the black hole inside a person's eyes. One whose eyes gaze into eternity will never look back at the former life, Moses leaving Egypt.

The universe's heart is in God, while the universe is the heart of God. The heart of the universe within us is the Spirit of God connected to the soul. The one who lives for God is at peace with the unknown. But what is known is what God reveals by his spoken Word through one's faith. You can only find God's peace through faith, but the faithfulness of God internally cannot be discovered from the outside eyes. Your eyes must glimpse God's glory from within without seeing signs and wonders from the outside world. One must experience the eternal signs and wonders. A blind man sees more of God than the eyes that see the world around them. A man that experiences God knows what they have been saved and delivered from. The soul that God has filled with the world is yet to discover the universe God created. The eyes without faith are a black hole sucking in the world, but the soul that walks by faith and not by sight sees the universe as a whole.

Jesus says it best in John 20:29, "because you have seen me, you have believed. Blessed are those who have not seen, yet believed." Those that see and believe with their spiritual eyes catch a glimpse of eternity. They close their physical eyes and see God's glory without the world's influence. They can be filled with the Spirit of God, receiving his grace and discovering his glory when they look into a mirror outwardly and inwardly, being open to God's Word and changing them with humility like Moses. They should see the reflection of Yeshua and the image of God in themselves. Paul says it best in 2 Corinthians 3:18, "But we all, with unveiled faces, looking as in a mirror at the glory of the Lord, are being transformed into the same image from glory to glory, just as from the Lord, the Spirit."

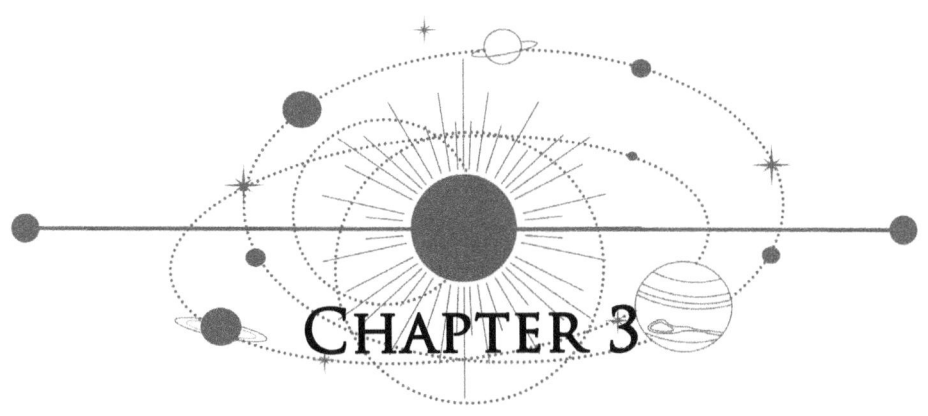

CHAPTER 3

The Purpose of Life

I often hear these words, "The world is much more wicked today than it was in ancient times." Historical records indicate that during biblical times Bible times and after those times were sacrifices (abortions) to Molech, sex with animals, and Canaanites committing pedophilia. There was worship of the moon, stars, sun, and idols of wood and stone. There were orgies and naked sex to Ishtar and Asherah. There was rape, murder, homosexuality, and even transgender people. One may be surprised to hear that there were transgender people even in ancient times. Egypt, Persia, Mesopotamia, and Babylon all had cross-dressers. Men dressed as women, and women dressed as men. Some men went as far as chopping off their genitals to resemble women like there are today. God commanded us in Deuteronomy 22 not to dress as the opposite sex, and Leviticus 18:22 says not to have sex with the same sex. Why? Because transgender people and homosexuals have been warring against God and defying the laws of nature since the fall of man. The reality is that it's always been wicked, yet we now have even more access to sin because it comes from our TVs, social media, phones, and the internet.

God gave us his laws to protect me from you and you from me. To protect us from each other and from ourselves. God wants to give us his peace. Lawlessness will defile and hurt our neighbor and hurt our relationship with God! Every homosexual or transgender I have ever met had something in common. Every single one has been sexually molested, raped, or physically abused. Many were in and out of foster homes where they went through abuse sexually, mentally, and physically. God's word proves that the damages outside His laws leave a lasting scar. His laws and words prove to be true. Every society and empire which has persisted with such actions above have fallen and ceased to exist. God will hear the cries of the innocent, suffering, and the righteous. But one must seek Him desperately if one wants salvation, like the prostitute Rahab. She trusted the word of God and the stories about the Israelites.

God has mercy on those He chooses according to their inner hearts. Notice I bring up the subject of the heart again, like in the previous chapter? God's word says He knows our heart and its intentions and desires. We can fool men, but we cannot fool God. He sees all things and knows all things. Nothing new occurs under the sun.

God wants to rescue and deliver those with humble, contrite hearts. He wants to save those who have sincere love and devotion. He will hear their cries and prayers and rescue them if they patiently and diligently await the Lord.

I often think about three men in prison. One spent his time saying, "I did no wrong. I must get out of here." while blaming the system or others. The second wants to leave prison while he plays sports, exercises, watches TV, plays games, fights with others, and is involved with prison gangs. The third admits, "I was wrong for my crimes, and I hope God will forgive me." He spent his days and nights praying, reading the Bible, and seeking God during his time. Which of these three people do you think God will justify before his throne?

Doesn't this sound like the parable of the seeds in Matthew 13? How much more will a seed that has died produce life? A seed that has not died, but fell off a tree like a leaf in the fall, will not produce life. Yeshua even said, "Most assuredly, I say to you, unless a grain of wheat falls into the ground and dies, it remains alone; but if it dies, it produces much grain." The incarcerated individual who sought divine guidance represents the seed that perished and bore fruit, signifying new life. Conversely, the remaining inmates lacked a genuine admission of wrongdoing and failed to express remorse or recognize the existence of a higher authority.

In Luke 18, the rich man looked at others and said, "God, I thank you that I am not like other people, robbers, evildoers, adulterers, or even like this tax collector." The tax collector wouldn't look up to heaven but beat his breast and said, 'God, have mercy on me, a sinner.' Who do you think will be justified before God? Take the two men on the cross beside Jesus—both committed crimes. One mocked him, and the other asked for repentance and believed he was the Messiah, even though all three were hanging from a cross! God told him, "You will surely be with me today in paradise."

Faith is all it takes, yet the Pharisees didn't believe. They were angry in Matthew 9 when Jesus healed the paralyzed man and told him, "Take courage, son; your sins have been forgiven." They called it blasphemy that Jesus would say, "Your sins are forgiven," not glorifying God that a paralyzed man could now walk! Nope! Instead, they were angry at Yeshua for healing the man! How much evil is within one's heart that someone would not want one to be forgiven or even healed spiritually or physically? Jesus even said to the Pharisees, "Why do you think evil in your hearts?"

Indeed, the Pharisees have not found forgiveness themselves because they did not have a humble and contrite heart to ask God for forgiveness. They did not acknowledge those sins nor take to heart their inner condition. Their heart was full of darkness without any light, for they would have recognized it if they had the light. As John 1:10 says, "He was in the world, and though the world was made through him, the world did not recognize him."

Remember I quoted the verse that God would destroy the wisdom of the wise? How much more today can one secretly not realize that they have religious pride or pride of knowledge, that they miss the light? When God becomes first, a heart judges itself and then ceases to point the finger at others—a heart after God desires healing, peace, and joy for every soul. One who doesn't long for such loving freedom for others has evil in their heart. There is likely a transgender person somewhere in the world that has a better chance of reaching repentance and entering God's kingdom than some pastors and churchgoers. Likewise, there is more hope for some women in the Netherlands' red light district than for some professing believers.

God knows the heart, just like he saved and delivered Rahab. He knows how to deliver each living soul in this world. God seeks out hearts full of justice, mercy, and compassion.

I often think back to a Jewish woman who told me a story about being in the Holocaust. A few Nazi soldiers injected her with unknown substances-a human test subject. She was also raped, beaten, and spit on. The Nazis murdered her parents, children, and siblings right before her eyes. As the years passed, she desired to meet those Nazi soldiers and talk with them. When she had her chance to meet them, she hugged and forgave them, and they broke into tears of sorrow and regret. What did this woman show? Mercy and compassion, full of the love of God who died for us, even while we were still sinners.

If the Bible was not true, where did that power come from that enabled that woman to hug and forgive those Nazis? It says in Acts 1:8, "You will receive power when the Holy Spirit comes on you," in Matthew 3:11, he will baptize us in spirit and fire. That fire will consume the sinful flesh, and the spirit of God will help us walk in the fruits of the spirit. It's a power to love, forgive, be holy, and live upright lives until the coming of Messiah, as Titus 2:11-15 states. Jesus says, "Love and pray for your enemies." He also says, "Forgive, and you will be forgiven," and "If you cannot forgive your enemies, your Father in heaven can't forgive you." The ultimate test in the vast journey of the wilderness in the universe, called life, is love and forgiveness. It's also the most challenging characteristic for many still full of themselves who cannot empty the polluted water from within.

Jesus says, "I am the way, the truth, and life; no man comes to the Father except through me" No one can truly find peace, rest, and contentment without discovering his ultimate plan of salvation and freedom. Yeshua says, "The gate is narrow, and few will find it, but the path to destruction is broad, and many will find it." But those who know his voice follow him wherever he goes, and he will keep them safe. Jesus says in Matthew 10:28, "Do not be afraid of those who kill the body but cannot kill the soul. Rather, be afraid of the One who can destroy both soul and body in hell." Like the Nazis, they could do incredible damage to someone's body but could not destroy their soul. No man can snatch God's children from his hands. We should fear the one who has power over our souls.

God has power over life and death. Jesus proved this power while walking on the earth and performing miracles. We are not to live in fear, for perfect love casts out all fear.

As we fully surrender to God, we begin living without fear, having God's peace, and walking more in the fruits of the spirit. I like to think of our walk with God like a plant growing inside us. Before that plant begins to grow, it must start with a seed. Until we come to know Yeshua, we will all have various seeds dropped within us. Some may have a hundred, while others may have ten. One seed may be from a pastor you heard a sermon from ten years ago and five more from someone who spoke to you in a grocery store. Another six or eight may be seeds from a family your kids made friends with within the neighborhood. Three or twenty seeds might be from a co-worker who shared Bible words while living as a light of God. Whatever the case or the instance in your life, the words you have remembered are a seed planted within you.

As time passes, one of those seeds may be ready to sprout with the right conditions in your life or the right word or message. You may have one of those former seeds within sprout up. That sprouting seed is the salvation of God that can grow and bear fruit. As it begins to be watered by the word of God and through faith, you will start to have other seeds grow. As other seeds grow, new seeds may plant as a garden in your soul begins to flourish. As Paul said in 1 Corinthians 3:6, "I planted the seed, Apollos watered it, but God has been making it grow."

If you think about your garden, someone planted a seed or multiple seeds, and several contributed to planting more. Someone may come along at the right time, which God uses, and then begin to water those seeds. God is the one who makes it grow, and it's up to us to take care of those plants. As verse 7 says, "So neither the one who plants nor the one who waters is anything, but only God, who makes things grow." It's not man's duty to help someone grow that plant, but rather God is the ultimate farmer and teacher.

Eventually, each human alive must choose to take care of their plants or let them die. The one who cares for the plants within their soul increases in God's wisdom, knowledge, and love. All of these combine to produce fruits of the spirit written in Galatians 5:22-24. When one is a small plant or a new believer, someone must teach them how to plant seeds and water them. But when one relies too much on a human being to teach them and becomes dependent after many years, they might overwater the plants causing them to die. One must learn to become dependent upon God and trust in him.

Please don't mistake my words. The Bible says a new believer was not to become a preacher. It protects them from falling into the same temptation as the devil, becoming prideful, seeking power, jealousy, and ultimately rebellion. Some twist the words written in 1 John 2:27, where it says that you don't need anyone to teach you. In context, that's about what is right and wrong, what is true and what is not. It has nothing to do with new believers not needing a teacher or each other. He's saying that God will give you discernment from the holy spirit and, with that discernment, will bring peace within one's soul. Discernment, wisdom, or knowledge without humility and love will become an internal pride. Be careful not to fall into the devil's snares, those who let pride creep in. They will waver like the sea waves tossing from one belief, religion, or theology to the next, never finding rest.

Let's proceed with our garden and seeds bearing fruit. Leviticus 19:23 says, "When you enter the land and plant any kind of fruit tree, regard its fruit as forbidden. For three years, you are to consider it forbidden; it must not be eaten." Yeshua himself repeats the words of Leviticus in a parable written in Luke 13:6-9 "A certain man had a fig tree planted in his vineyard, and he came seeking fruit on it and found none. Then he said to the keeper of his vineyard, 'Look, for three years, I have come seeking fruit on this fig tree and find none. Cut it down; why does it use up the ground?' But he answered and said to him, 'Sir, let it alone this year also until I dig around it and fertilize it. And if it bears fruit, well. But if not, after that, you can cut it down." Yeshua gives an example; it takes an average of 3 years with hunger and thirst for his righteousness. The person is adequately trained diligently in God's ways. Even Paul, Timothy, Silas, and others would teach communities and congregations. In my profession in ministry and my walk with God for many years, I can witness many people coming to know God within the first three years and then departing to another mixture of various doctrines, beliefs, or faith. It all combines bits and pieces of various seeds and gardens.

This example reminds me of the Torah in Deuteronomy 22:9-11 when God says not to mix seeds. People are mixing seeds of various beliefs believing they lead to the seed of life. Instead, it comes from the corrupted seed of the forbidden fruit. People eat and grow it in their gardens because it looks and tastes good. One can receive many seeds, but is it from the holy spirit that produces good fruits? Are bad seeds poisoning the soul and creating death within an individual?

It reminds me of edible blueberries but then coming across poisonous privet berries. They look similar to the eye, but one produces life, and the other produces death. Likewise, the holy spirit produces life, and sin produces death. While some things may look similar, they could be a familiar spirit rather than the holy one. You will know based on how much love, forgiveness, mercy, compassion, humility, kindness, and peace you have inside. If you ever feel those things leaving, evaluate your heart to see if you live in willful sin. If you are not living in willful sin, assess the direction you may be going in or what you may be listening to.

Paul repeats similar writing when speaking to Timothy. 2 Timothy 2:13 "But evil men and imposters will go from bad to worse, deceiving and being deceived." While he wrote more in 2 Timothy 3:10, "You, however, closely followed my teaching, manner of life, purpose, faithfulness, patience, love, perseverance." If you retain those characteristics, you will be safe until the end. Hold fast to the condition in which you first found Jesus.

Over the years, I have heard hundreds of times, "When I first came to know Jesus, I was on fire, and I felt amazing. But now I feel like I have no fire and can't feel God." I always ask, "What is your daily life like? How do you spend your week?" The repeated response is, "I try to pray and read, but I'm just so busy." The answer is right in front of their eyes.

Every human alive on this earth has 24 hours in a day. The average person works eight hours, sleeps eight hours, and is free for eight hours. If Daniel was a busy man working for the government in Babylon, in charge of many people, how did he still find time to pray three times a day? What we love, we make a priority for, and what we desire, we put our energy towards doing it. Living for God is neither a feeling nor faith based on a feeling. One day you may feel happy, while another, you may feel mad or depressed. If you felt angry or depressed one day, do you believe it would be harder to feel love? Would you feel like serving another? What about long weeks or months of depression or anger? Wouldn't you feel abandoned and unloved if you didn't hear from God or if your spouse gave you no attention during those more challenging times? Love can not live on feelings. Love is a verb and an action.

We might not feel like praying, reading, or giving our spouse a hug or a massage, but we must understand that faith and love go beyond how we feel. Faith is something we hope for, yet we can not see it. We hope our marriage will last. We also hope for Yeshua to save us on the last day. Although we can't see 20 years from now in one's marriage nor see Yeshua physically, we hope, pray, and trust that we will. The things we love, we make an effort to act upon.

I recall a man who used to leave his blinds open in his home. He would come home from work and, like clockwork, flip on the TV and begin watching sports until lights out. That was what he desired. It was his love and his passion. Others may enjoy other hobbies or activities to stimulate the mind and senses. I will repeat it, whatever a human loves, they will put effort into spending time doing it. If you love your spouse, you will want to do things with them and talk with them. If you love your dog, you will love playing with them, petting them, and caring for them. Likewise, those who love God will enjoy praying, reading, sitting in his presence, listening, and talking to him.

If we journey back to the subject of your garden and its plants, you will be diligent about carefully learning to care for your plants and garden. One with a garden of their own will want to learn all about the crops they're growing. If one is growing tomatoes, cucumbers, or string beans, wouldn't you want to ensure the plants bring forth the best-tasting vegetables? Wouldn't you want to ensure it is nutrient-dense, flavorful, and without bugs or rotting mold? Doesn't a gardener pull out the weeds, fertilize, prune, and tend to each growing plant? In the same way, think about the word of God as one giant seed. When you come to repent of your sins and believe in Yeshua, the growing seed will take a lifetime of learning from God to grow into a fruitful tree.

Suppose you take the words of Yeshua in Mark 4:30-32. "How should we picture the kingdom of God? Or by what story shall we present it? It is like a mustard seed when it's planted in the ground. Though the smallest of all seeds in the earth, yet when planted, it grows up and becomes the largest of all the herbs. It puts forth big branches, so the birds of the air can nest in its shade." If you don't take time to learn to grow that plant, how will it give shade to the root and give its rest to people? When Yeshua said that unless you become born again, you will not enter the kingdom of heaven. He also says the kingdom of heaven God is for those who become like little children. What exactly is he saying?

Think about coming to know Christ. One must be born again and emptied of themselves so that his holy spirit will come to live with them.

One can't be a year old and suddenly turn fifty. Likewise, a baby can't drink milk from the breast or a bottle and suddenly devour a steak. What will happen if you feed a baby steak? That's right. The baby will choke, and so will each individual who is the same spiritually. Paul also was speaking to people who skipped applesauce and the toddler stages. Hebrews 5:12 says, "In fact, though by this time you ought to be teachers, you need someone to teach you the elementary truths of God's word all over again. You need milk, not solid food!" If we skip the proper steps designed by God's purpose and plan, we will miss what God is trying to teach and show us.

A child in elementary school learning to read and write can't suddenly go to college and begin medical or law school, can they? So why would anyone who begins to read or write in God's school suddenly believe they can become a judge or surgeon? It's dangerous to become a judge too quickly and catastrophic if one becomes a surgeon too fast.

If you skip patient endurance with God, you will become prideful. It's like the news story in Florida with all those nurses receiving fake diplomas. How many medical errors would occur to their patients because of a fake diploma and improper training? Likewise, the soul that becomes too full of knowledge and skips growing up with God can become prideful and be a danger to others. Even more, they can cause harm to themselves.

Growing a plant takes time before the crops can yield their fruit. When the fruit has yielded its produce, it matures and takes time to ripen. It tastes delightful only when someone picks the fruits early enough and at the right time. If someone collects the fruit too late, they fall off and rot. If someone gleans the fruit at the right time, they taste great and will be enjoyed by those who eat them. One who takes time to mature with God will be nutritious and pleasant to the senses. Their fruits will proceed to the soul's stomach and digest the nutrition of God's truth and grace. One's fruits picked too early and haven't taken enough time to grow with God will produce bitterness to others and their senses. It will cause the body to pucker up and the mouth and soul to spit it up.

The one picked too late stopped caring for their garden. They became rotten and disgusting to the senses, and the soul and the stomach wanted to vomit upon tasting them. If you are reading this and still need clarification, I will explain it in simpler terms. I am speaking about people's lives and their souls within them. The early crops lack endurance, perseverance, patience, forgiveness, understanding, and wisdom. The overripe crops lack humility, kindness, love, faithfulness, obedience, compassion, and self-control. In contrast, the crops that are just right have love, joy, peace, patience, generosity, faith, and self-control. They are those who God leads by the spirit rather than the impulses and works of the flesh.

Matthew 13 goes into greater depth regarding the various individuals and the seeds that they received. Whether seeds of eternal life living for God or seeds for the temporary life living for the world. Yeshua's sacrifice brings you back into the garden as if it were Genesis 2:15 before returning. "The Lord God took the man and put him in the Garden of Eden to work it and take care of it." Eden is your soul saved by God's holy spirit. The garden is the earth, and the plants are within you to produce fruit until we receive our glorified bodies at Yeshua's coming. He is reversing the damage that sin and the tainted earth have done. It's as if we are all polluted with toxic GMO seeds, but God has removed them and replaced them with organic seeds within our souls. While he continues to reverse the damage done to our bodies through sanctification, he is restoring the soul that has received the incorruptible seed. As 1 Peter 1:23 says, "For you have been born again, not of perishable seed, but of imperishable, through the living and enduring word of God." As we continue with what Yeshua prayed for us in John 17:17, "Sanctify them in truth, for your word is truth." As we read in Galatians 2:20, "I have been crucified with Yeshua. It is no longer I who live, but Messiah who lives in me. And the life I now live in the flesh, I live by faith in the Son of God, who loved me and gave himself for me." As Paul wrote in 1 Thessalonians 5:23, "May the God of peace make you completely holy. May your entire spirit, soul, and body be kept blameless for the coming of our Lord Yeshua the Messiah."

CHAPTER 4

What Is Life

L ife is full of mysteries, questions, and wonder. There will be small and large mountains to climb throughout one's life. I often reflect on my travels through the Appalachian Mountains in Tennessee and Georgia. Those mountains are small compared to the Rocky Mountains of Colorado, Canada, or the Swiss Alps of Switzerland. Not only will it take your breath away upon seeing them, but it will also take your breath away by hiking them. Throughout your own life, it will be like those mountains. Upon entering the hills, you travel through the vast wilderness and rocky cliffs before traveling to the tallest peaks. There will be some smaller hills and valleys before reaching larger ones. As you continue your journey, you'll encounter smaller valleys and hills that will provide relief.

I frequently reminisce about my experiences kayaking and river rafting through the challenging summer Olympic rapids. Before reaching those rapids, there were calm waters before the heavy raging waters. The rapids would be so strong that they could flip you upside down. But after the entire journey of the calm before more rapids, there was peace and exhilarating joy in accomplishing those rapids. Our life is similar to those rapids and those mountains to climb. Sometimes, the struggle, suffering, hardships, and pain can be relatable to all those travels. But while we overcome those rapids or hike 5000' to 14,000' mountains, we can ask ourselves, what is this purpose?

When one hikes a cliff, they know the motivation behind why they are doing it. Likewise, one who jumps in a kayak or a raft and embarks out on a river with raging rapids knows why they're doing it. Why not ask yourself the same question? Why am I going through this? What is my purpose? What is God trying to show me? For instance, think about a bird flying from tree to tree while eating worms on the ground. What is their purpose in life, and why? Many seek their most significant internal and life purpose and must discover the meaning. If a celebrity becomes rich and famous by obtaining that success from their choices and actions contrary to God, is this the definition of holy? Is it a design and purpose by God?

One can take a dart board positioned 25' to 50' away and throw a dart until it hits the bullseye. Someone can say, "I hit the mark! I know my purpose in life!" But if someone has never played darts, throwing the dart and hitting the bullseye the first time, it's not unlikely that it will ever happen without first throwing tens, if not hundreds to thousands of throws, before hitting the bullseye.

In your own life, you can believe in your mind that the will of God is that bullseye. But if you miss the first time, why would you keep throwing darts to hit the bullseye, knowing that's not the will of God? Success and riches in this life are neither the things we can tangibly obtain nor are money, position, power, fame, starting a prospering business, or climbing the career ladder at your job. That's the bullseye at which one had to throw darts many times to succeed. It's likely not the purpose and will of God, but rather to be content with him. Success is living for God and utilizing your time to grow more in his image. The riches are loving and helping your neighbor, living a life of dignity, and respect for yourself and others. It's a life full of the spirit of God prospering in your soul rather than the abundance of this Earth.

The Nile River in Egypt symbolized wealth and prosperity, yet God turned it into blood. The river of the world intersects with Babylon through asphalt streets, highways, and interstates: high-rising buildings, elaborate and sophisticated houses with all the luxury, bells, and whistles. People strive for cars, clothes, and toys in their garages. But even with that river flowing into one's driveway or place of residence, it's a river full of blood and vanity! God says in Revelation that Babylon was full of the blood of righteous saints who are God's people. Do you want your blood floating in the Nile river of your life connected to Babylon? What flows from the heart flows streams out into the world. What the hand desires reveals the soul within a man. Like California's San Andreas fault line, the world's empire is cracking at its foundation. Eventually, the mighty shaking will come, and the kingdom will collapse like Rome in a single day.

The achievement of man is garbage to the man in the grave. A moving truck has no business for the body in a coffin. Likewise, everything you have obtained in this life will go to another or end up in a landfill. As Solomon quotes in Ecclesiastes 6:2, "God gives some people wealth, possessions and honor, so that they lack nothing their hearts desire, but God does not grant them the ability to enjoy them, and strangers enjoy them instead. This is meaningless, a grievous evil."

What purpose does one have if they have obtained the world yet sold their soul? You might quickly respond, "That's not me; that's for people like the celebrity." But even a sanitation worker driving a truck can sell his soul to the job without ever seeking and spending time with God. The quote is valid, "the dead doesn't know they're living, and the living doesn't know they're dead." I once said it in a sermon, hitting me like a pile of bricks. The dead don't know they're living in the afterlife to come, whether heaven or hell. The living doesn't realize they're dead and living for the things in the world. The way you live on Earth is a test before leaving. BIBLE stands for "Basic Instructions Before Leaving Earth."

I mentioned earlier that nothing can destroy our souls. When the Israelites were in ancient Egypt as enslaved people, God told them before Passover to put the lamb's blood on the doorpost of their homes. The blood resembles the humble, contrite, obedient, and repentant souls that neither conform to Egypt nor love its lifestyle. This story represents the future blood of the lamb, Yeshua, the sacrifice for us all. All people with the lamb's blood on their hearts, sealed by God, will be passed over from worldly and eternal plagues. Just like the doorposts in Egypt. Is the blood of the lamb covering the doorposts of your hearts? God commands the Israelites to write his laws on their doorposts and have them in their hearts and minds. That comes through the work of the new covenant through the holy spirit. We should engrave his mark and seal on our life, forehead, and actions representing our right hand.

Likewise, the mark of the beast is everything contrary to the will of God and his design and purpose. It's immorality, along with all lusts and pleasures of the world like Egypt. False worship of foreign gods, and every ounce of idolatry and apostasy that will cast you away from the living, true God. The blasphemy of the spirit is simply a total rejection of God and not allowing the holy spirit's work to rule and bring change in your life. God saved and delivered the Israelites out of Egypt, who obeyed and listened to his word. The spirit of death and misery visited the ones who failed to receive the word. Death and pain represent what will happen to all who fail to receive the word of the living God. Those who repent and live holy by faith receive the gift of eternal life. The choice is yours, for each one of us. Whether to live and see within the box or allow God to carry one out of the box.

Egypt, Persia, Mesopotamian, Rome, Greece, and Babylon are inside the box. It's all of the influences and designs of the world combined into one. Now reflect and remember the box I spoke about at the beginning of this book. God tested the Israelites to see if they were authentic, like hiking the mountains and going through the rapids. They would have entered the promised land within the first couple of months. Yet they were not faithful, nor did they have trust. Even though they tasted the good fruits of the land, they claimed to see giants and became afraid. Those giants represent the sin and obstacles in our life. What keeps us from having a pure heart and relationship with God, and causes us fear, shame, or guilt, is the giant in our life!

Although one may have tasted the good fruits of God's kingdom and received his son Yeshua, one may still have to overcome the giants and the rough terrain before discovering greater faith and peace. One who chooses the dart board life may have it easy, like driving the roads through the mountains or walking along the river on paved roads. They may never see the sights or know the path outside the paved roads. They will never grasp life's slow journey outside of the fast-paced travel inside the car.

One who chooses the fastest method will always suffer a more significant loss. Though one may be successful by the world's standards, in what seems to be an overnight success; the loss of inner originality and the sight of a fruitful reality becomes dim and blurry. Losing oneself is the greatest bankruptcy, more disruptive than an entire stock market and housing crash. One who loses sight of the life yet to come forfeits incredible success within one's soul.

All the riches are robbed and rusted. The inner man is like the Titanic wasting away at the bottom of the sea. It's unable to be restored and utilized again. The soul, married to the world's cruise ship liners, will eventually sink while drowning other lives they have influenced. The influence of one's soul tainted by the world, with eyes set on its allurements, has cut off entire generations and offspring. The greatest killer in the world is not abortion, medicines, or guns. The greatest killer is a soul who the world's attractions have purchased. One who has given themselves over to slavery of religion, politics, sports, business, education, and money. One who has forgotten that there is a world beyond the dartboard, who has not seen behind the wall in which the dartboard hangs. The desires of one's heart have overrun the target in one's mind.

The Bible says that the heart is deceitful above all things; who can trust it? Our desires can become aligned with the world's desires. It may be a parent, friend, sibling, co-worker, a bad breakup, a divorce, a TV show, or social media that has influenced our behavior, desires, or will for our choices and actions in this life. But does one know the reasoning behind it, or are they just telling themselves that this is God's will for their life? Let's look back on Adam and Eve. They desired to become wise like God, knowing good and evil, and didn't want to die. After God told them not to eat from the Tree of Knowledge of Good and Evil, they knew of death and didn't want to die. Then the serpent used their fears against them and enticed them with what they desired. We have now become a fallen people because of the knowledge of evil. It has always been God's will for us to have peace with him.

Ultimately, it was the greatest loss humanity has ever faced and caused devastation to millions of offspring and generations afterward. So terrible that we are still seeing the results of one person's actions today. Think about your own life. Are you thinking like Adam and Eve? Or is your thinking based on eternity and the coming kingdom of God? Jesus says, "Be perfect as I am perfect." In the Greek context, it means morally perfect. What is morally and ethically pure? His holiness, grace, mercy, faithfulness, goodness, justice, and righteousness. It's also the fruits of His spirit written in Galatians 5:22-24. It's who he is. It's giving Him your devotion, obedience, love, and worship. One can praise anything in this life, but what about worship? One can praise their kids, a co-worker, an athlete at a sports event, and even their dog or cat. One will praise another when they have won their validation or done something commending or well done. But worship involves our entire being with complete respect, devotion, and honor. It involves your whole heart, soul, and will. One can worship their job until they get laid off or fired. One may worship their kids until they grow up or do something that disappoints them in total rebellion. One might worship the creation by giving in to wanderlust and spending their entire lives exploring this Earth. One may worship money yet not realize it also receives so much devotion and honor.

In fact, people can worship anything or anyone, just as they can praise anything or anyone. All of one's desires can become worship. Do you enjoy the above things? Evaluate if you worship God or the created. Do your sincerely worship and praise God or the things in the world? Life is a journey and a process. There is no easy button to finish the task. Life is like computer programming and engineering. It takes a vast amount of coding with trial and error. A computer programmer devotes to learning the language and coding until it successfully connects without errors or bugs. Likewise, we are continually learning the language of God until the bugs and errors in our lives are fixed, removed, and resolved. God wants us to operate and perform efficiently so that he may use the programming within us to run smoothly and effectively. God knows that even the best computers and programs still have issues. That's why we all need updates within our motherboards.

I am speaking of the brain here. The more we understand and comprehend God, the more we begin to operate on his server. When we act on his server and his coding, we can be more beneficial for God running by his design. Exactly how he intended our design for his creation. For instance, think about the latest computer programs in some healthcare settings. Without it, they would not be able to function as a hospital, and the results of the malfunctions would be devastating within all of their hospital facilities. If we don't upgrade and continually grow with God, the effects will be just as devastating. You might as well operate from a first-generation Mac computer and try to sell it to hospitals. Telling them "to utilize its technology because it's a major scientific breakthrough," but you won't get too far. Who would want 1980s technology in a life or death situation when we have an even more remarkable breakthrough of technology in healthcare, with a greater chance of survival?

If we cease to live for God, we might as well view ourselves as the first generation Mac or a Windows 95, 2000, or XP operating system without an upgrade. Many people upgrade their phones frequently to acquire the latest edition of the iPhone or Android to meet the status quo in society. Yet often, one does not upgrade their heart and mind to function and operate by God's design. Most of humanity is like the latest edition of smartphones or computer gadgets, yet the soul is like an old Windows or Mac computer. Many are okay with upgrading to keep up with modern times and allow the world's design to shape and mold them. Contrary, when it comes to changing within one's soul to act according to God's ultimate will and plan and being molded into God's image, that becomes too difficult.

If God commands us to bear fruit in keeping with repentance, what can we understand from this? God can change anyone from the inside, and our will can take the form of holy living. God is the same as yesterday, today, and forever. The nature of God is not outdated. When we accept Yeshua as our Lord and Savior, our soul finds the upgrade in his kingdom while the flesh grows older and outdated. God knows our flaws and can change the coding in our souls to operate within his server in his kingdom.

What one sees in the mirror is different from how one views themselves. The statement "We are each our own worst critic" is true.

Every human alive will see attractive physical traits and major physical flaws looking at their body in a mirror. Likewise, how one sees the mirror within often differs from how they see their physical self. Each of us will see negative qualities and positive qualities. We will see things that we like and things that we don't like. Some will miss a lot within themselves because they are too focused on one part. For instance, one woman may be caught up in their makeup and covering up minor blemishes, whereas a man may become focused on their arm muscles or abs not being cut or big enough. If one recognizes the outward flaws they dislike, how much more should one focus on the internal flaws?

One who lives for God will see extraordinary internal qualities. The lunar eclipse within our hearts will come to light bursting forth with the positivity and respect of yourself. The darkened negative qualities that are seen or not seen will shine like a bright sunny day. One will begin to think, see, and act differently in their conduct. Jesus says, "I am the light of the world. Whoever follows me will never walk in darkness but will have the light of life." He tells us that he will remove negative qualities, and the light will burst forth with positive ones. Yeshua tells us that "the eye is the lamp to the soul, but if the eye is bad, the whole body will be full of darkness. But if the eye is full of light, the whole body will be full of light." He then tells us that "we cannot serve two masters." We can't serve God and money. We can't serve God and the world. We cannot live like an old first cell phone called the Hagenuk Global Handy while looking like the latest iPhone. God wants us to upgrade according to his plan and design while resembling him. We aren't trying to look and operate like the newest cell phone on the market made by humans. We want to be programmed and look like God's design made by him.

In 1 Samuel 16:7, God told Samuel that he doesn't look at physical appearance but rather the heart. The heart and mind are the two most unexplored regions in the universe. An echocardiogram and MRI can see images, but they cannot tell us the spiritual condition of the soul connected to both. Proverbs 4:23 says, "Above all else, guard your heart, for everything you do flows from it." The heart is full of emotions, desires, passions, and will. If David was a man after God's heart, what were his emotions, desires, passions, and will set on? David focused his seat of emotions and desires on God. His appetite became satiated with the presence and word of God. He hungered not for the bread we can physically admire with our five senses but rather the bread of life that comes from above, satiating and nourishing one's soul. He thirsted for righteousness and to have God's presence close and near.

At Ein Gedi, David wasn't concerned about the water to drink. He was concerned about loving his enemy Saul and resting with God. That reveals loving God with all of your heart, soul, and understanding and loving your neighbor as yourself. The very two pillars hold up all the other laws God gave since the foundation of creation. Yeshua repeats, "On these two commandments, hang all the law and the prophets." I like to call a heart without God spiritual heart failure. While the mind, without God, is a brain that is spiritually dead.

In medical terms, a diagnosis of being braindead or having heart failure equates to death. How much more is death within the soul that has yet to discover the incredible infinite truths and wisdom of God's amazing grace and mercy? How can we know if we are right before God? The answer is revealed within 1 John 3:21 "Beloved if our heart does not condemn us, we have confidence before God." If we have no guilt within us, and we have repented from sin, one can be confident to approach the spiritual prayer altar of God. As Philippians 4:7 says, "And the peace of God, which surpasses all comprehension, will guard your hearts and your minds in Christ Jesus." Let our confidence be in him, with great peace and without guilt and shame.

CHAPTER 5.

Create Me Clean and Pure

I was walking through the wilderness in the Rocky Mountains of America. Suddenly, I heard David's words in Psalm 51 speaking loudly and clearly through my head, saying, "Create in me a clean heart, O God; and renew a right spirit within me. Cast me not away from your presence, and take not your holy spirit from me." It began to grow louder into a symphony of opera houses. I began to hear and see the voices and multitudes of what sounded like and appeared to be millions of people. All were crying out for the Messiah as my soul desperately longed for this within my entire being. Later, I thought back on the great musician Keith Green who sincerely loved God, as he performed this song to a crowd of others. I recall the wonderful preacher Leonard Ravenhill and how often he would mention his music and close friendship. Both have had a tremendous impact on the believing community throughout the world.

God used Leonard Ravenhill immensely as he would spend eight to ten hours praying every day for over a year with a group of men. Out of that came some of the most spirit-filled revivals within the individual souls of men and women throughout the nations.

While reflecting upon all these thoughts, I heard, "Cast me not away from thy presence; and take not thy holy spirit from me. Restore unto me the joy of thy salvation, and uphold me with thy free spirit." How desperately does my soul cry from the spirit of God, long for these things? Later one day, I sat in the shower, forgetting about that time as I prayed unceasingly. These wonderful and powerful words once again cried out from the deepest crevices of my entire being. As I sang these words unto God, a mixture of both joy and sadness filled me internally. I thought, Adonai, my Lord, how impure is my heart? How unclean are my thoughts?

The cry of Psalms 102:1-2 spoke louder in my heart than in a championship sports arena with a tied game at the last minute. I cry out, "Hear my prayer, Lord! And let my cry for help come to you. Do not hide Your face from me on the day of my distress! Incline Your ear to me! On the day when I call, answer me quickly." God loves it when we rely on him and seek his face. Jeremiah 29:13 says, "You will seek me and find me when you seek me with all your heart." Sometimes we don't always hear from God when we expect to. Daniel is an excellent example of this in Daniel 10:12-13. He continued to pray and seek the face of God, then an angel eventually replied to him and said God heard his prayer. But there was a war in the heavens, and the angel could not deliver the message.

When we pray to God, the devil and his demons must also hear the prayers going up to the heavens. After all, why do praying men and women sometimes have more spiritual battles?

In the same way, someone who speaks about God to others while sharing the gospel will likely receive more spiritual battles. The devil is not threatened by someone who lives like the world and for the world because he has already got them where he wants them. He is threatened by those living for God, those set apart from the world while living for holiness. Job is another example of living for righteousness and prayers that took a long time for God to answer, which could have been decades.

Job, a man who lost his wife, ten children, and his friends were against him. He lost all of his livestock which were one's finances and food during those times. Then he was struck with illness, great suffering, and pain. God allowed the devil to test him beyond reasons we may not always know. But even through all of his suffering, he continued to seek God. In Job 1:21, he says, "Naked I came from my mother's womb, And naked I shall return there. The Lord gave, and the Lord has taken away. Blessed be the name of the Lord." That's incredible faith! Even if Job himself had some flaws, some parts of him believed to know all about God. In the end, God answered him in such a powerful way it diminished that pride within his soul. Though we read from the beginning of Job's life, before disaster and hardship came upon him, Job carefully sacrificed often, even sacrificing on account of his children. People respected, revered, and honored Job greatly. Job didn't care about wealth, power, or the praise of others. Job lived for God and honored him with his careful lifestyle and conduct. What about you? Are you careful in the conduct of your life pleasingly to God?

Romans 12:1 says, "Therefore I urge you, brothers and sisters, by the mercies of God, to present your bodies as a living and holy sacrifice, acceptable to God, which is your spiritual service of worship." And Romans 5:2-5 says, "tribulation produces perseverance; and perseverance, character; and character, hope. Now hope does not disappoint because the Love of God has been poured out in our hearts by the Holy Spirit who was given to us." We learn by perseverance, like Job or the Israelites in the desert. It is to test one's character. Your character resembles the nature of who God is. When one perseveres and has the character of God, it then produces hope and the Love of God. As 1 Corinthians 13:4-7 says, "Love is patient, Love is kind. It does not envy; it does not boast. It is not proud. It does not dishonor others; it is not self-seeking, it is not easily angered, and it keeps no record of wrongs. Love does not delight in evil but rejoices with the truth. It always protects, always trusts, always hopes, always perseveres."

Self-seeking takes pleasure in the world, and dishonoring others lacks respect and kindness. Unforgiveness of one another keeps records of wrongs. It holds grudges and destroys the inner soul. Someone easily angered does not resemble the character of God, which is the fruit of the spirit, with all kindness, gentleness, and humility. One that delights in sin cannot rejoice in the truth of God. 1 John 3:6 says, "No one who lives in Him keeps on sinning. No one who continues to sin has either seen Him or known Him." As 1 John 2:4 says, "He who says, "I know Him," and does not keep His commandments, is a liar, and the truth is not in him." As 1 John 4:8 says, "Whoever does not love does not know God, because God is love." We know that Love never fails and that perfect Love casts out all fear, but let's see what else Paul mentions about Love.

1 Corinthians 13:8 "Love never fails. But where there are prophecies, they will cease; where there are tongues, they will be stilled; where there is knowledge, it will pass away." All the gifts of the spirit, all of one's intellect, and all of one's skills will pass away. What will not pass away is the Love of God and the Love that overcomes the world. Just as Yeshua has overcome the world, his spirit also gave us the power to overcome the world. He has given us the power to rule over the flesh, which craves the world and its behavior. God wants us to have internal Peace while living in the world. As John 14:27 says, "Peace I leave with you; my Peace I give you. I do not give to you as the world gives. Do not let your hearts be troubled, and do not be afraid." Jesus prayed this over everyone, past and present, who will come to believe in him, and that also come to know his saving grace.

I like to imagine our lives are like a ship or boat in the ocean. The first ship is a cruise ship. Everything is fun, easy, smooth sailing, and full of amusements, entertainment, food, and activities. The second is a battleship, where you may have smooth sailing. But at other times, it's war, work, hardship, rough waters, and uncertainty. It might not always be on the edge. There can still be times of laughter and fun.

I recall having the opportunity to explore a naval ship at a military port in Norfolk, Virginia. It was no bells and whistles, neither luxurious nor comfortable. The ship was full of gray and blue painted steel, metal, and flooring. I recall very few activities. There were free weights, board games, a TV, and a Spalding basketball goal. The bunk beds looked uncomfortable and cold. The kitchen looked like an old high school cafeteria. While on the ship, I observed the vast amounts of weaponry stored on it. Although the vessel was not visually appealing, it could weather the storms and remove the enemy.

I preferred to avoid the activities offered on a cruise ship. I wasn't concerned with the casinos, concerts, or Broadway-style plays. I did not enjoy hanging out around the outdoor pools, which felt chaotic, busy, and worldly. People were drinking alcohol everywhere, and the noise was overwhelming. So much laughter, screams, talking, and noise from the crowds and activities around the ship. Many people tried to appear wealthy, flashy, or better than others around them. I rather enjoyed the room, sitting on the balcony, and enjoying the breeze and the sight of the neverending water.

It was always the finer region of the country when the ship would reach its destination. The crowds were overwhelmed by the sites, and people would walk around saying, "Wow, this is beautiful!" They would shop, do a few dedicated activities nearby, rest on the beach, drink, and eat. What was incredible to me was that no one paid attention to what was happening around the rest of the country. No one paid it any mind, nor did anyone show concern. Maybe someone did somewhere, but what I observed felt like a distraction from reality. Poverty, suffering, sickness, death, and violence were all ignored.

On the cruise ship of one's life, one may have fun, entertainment, and activities. But they are distracted from the one who created human life, the oceans, and the land God created from the sea. The battleships, on the other hand, are not for the weak and fearful. One must be tough as steel, focused, dedicated, and always prepared for action. Paul says in 2 Timothy 4:2, "Preach the word! Be ready in season and out of season. Convince, rebuke, exhort, with all longsuffering and teaching." Living with God takes the endurance and perseverance of a battleship. We should always be prepared for action in the spiritual and physical world. Preparing inwardly and outwardly for whatever life may bring your way. In Ephesians 6:13, Paul writes, "Therefore take up the whole armor of God, that you may be able to withstand in the evil day, and having done all, to stand firm."

In the military, every soldier alive would like to go home to see their family. How much more should one living for God take their walk seriously in suiting up and preparing for battle when we see Him? When someone in the military decides to enlist in the branch of their choice, they first take a written test to see whether they can pass. Then based on their intelligence and physical performance, it's determined where the soldier will be positioned in the army. God does the same thing with us. He tests us to see if we can pass the test before placing us in certain positions in his army.

Each person who enlists in the military attends basic beginner's training. Upon arrival, you will have a drill instructor yelling and screaming in everyone's faces. The instructor is conditioning you to be a strong soldier. They start by breaking down the weakness inside so that their soldiers unite and, as a result, become well-trained. God does the same with us. He first shakes out all our sins and strengthens us. Things that are deep inside that don't belong or hinder our faith. God will remove our fear, worry, weakness, doubts, and anxiety. We will then begin to operate and function together in unity within the body of Messiah.

I think about those who advance in training or move into specialized training for the chosen position or what they have selected. They must undergo the proper training, just like joining God's army. Imagine if a recruit skipped basic training and the commander immediately gave a uniform, firearm, boots, and helmet, then sent his army into war? What impact would that have on each soldier and others around him? Can you imagine a new believer in Christ who has never faced trial and error or was never taught and trained by a professional? Then suddenly were sent out to evangelize, sent out as a missionary, lead as a pastor, or go out and live in the world. How do you think that would affect that individual and those around them? It would devastate the mind, body, and soul of someone not adequately trained for life or war.

A soldier who goes through training is ready for the battleship, but one who has not gone through the training has lived on a cruise ship. Today the church appears to act, live, and look like a cruise ship. Can you imagine, in America, minorities who are lowering the test score standards to accommodate an entire culture or race?

It's happening today. Minorities can now become doctors and surgeons more easily. Can you imagine someone passing tests to become a brain surgeon that would typically not have passed if they were not a minority? Would you want that person operating on your brain or your child's brain if there was a cancerous tumor? Of course not! Then why would we want men and women telling us about God's word that has not accurately passed the test called life? John 10:1 says, "Very truly I tell you Pharisees, anyone who does not enter the sheep pen by the gate, but climbs in by some other way, is a thief and a robber."

Yeshua is the gate. There is no other way to enter. One must pass the test. There are no free handouts. There are no games like Monopoly to collect $500, pass go, and get out of jail free cards. God wants soldiers adequately trained. He wants us to work together in unity as one. If your arm or leg has a medical condition called paresthesia, numbness, tingling, and prickling of the limb, do you think you will play any sports or fight in battle? Of course not! So we want to ensure we are functioning together as a whole. Not just as an individual in heart, soul, and mind but also as the body of believers. Like America's Army motto, "Army Strong!" We must be "Heaven Strong!" You cannot enlist in the military if you have certain medical conditions. Likewise, someone with willful sins and disobedience cannot join God's army.

How will one resist and fight against the demons, worldly influences, and enticements of sin? To put it simply, they cannot. Their body is weak. They fight with broken armor. The gates and barriers of their soul have been torn down. If you were to buy a home and build a fence, would you want it to fall apart once installed? What about a house with surprise repairs that will suddenly drain your bank account? Why would you come to Jesus, then quickly allow the world to break down your fence? Why would you come to know Yeshua, then live a life in sin, which costs a lifetime and an abundance of resources to repair? God wants you to be well-equipped and prepared for life, regardless of the journey.

Suppose some people know that a big category-five hurricane is coming to Florida or another island. Wouldn't they be wise to prepare sandbags, generators, life vests, food, water, and other essential survival gear? Those who do not prepare may be swept away, like fish for shark bait. When one prepares with God, one will be ready for spiritual storms and weather conditions. The trained and prepared soul will have character, endurance, perseverance, and hope for God's kingdom. Like Job, he was ready for the battle when the war and storms hit physically and spiritually. He received scrapes, bumps, and bruises throughout the struggle; nevertheless, he overcame the power of God through perseverance and endurance. Despite suffering, pain, loss, and great sorrow, he kept his faith in God.

The tribulation will come in this life. As my father said, "It's not a matter of IF hardship will happen; it's a matter of WHEN." James 1:12 says, "Blessed is the one who perseveres under trial because, having stood the test, that person will receive the crown of life that the Lord has promised to those who love him." If you were a runner in the Olympics competing in the 100-meter hurdles, would you not give it your all to overcome those hurdles and win the race? How much more can we view life's hurdles like that race in the Olympics?

On national television, I see those athletes proud of their accomplishments when receiving the gold medal. How much more will one rejoice in accepting the crown of life for overcoming those hurdles and winning the race of life? Remember in John 16:33, Jesus says we will have tribulation in this life? The tribulation means troubles or hardships, but after he says that when these things occur, you might have Peace in me. He says, "Take heart! I have overcome the world." Let this be an encouraging word to take heart, and do not fear! Ponder upon these words within your heart and mind.

Deuteronomy 31:6 "Be strong and courageous. Do not be afraid or terrified because of them, for the Lord your God goes with you; he will never leave you or forsake you." If we read back on the times of Israel before the war, the military leader encouraged the people that God was with them and not to be afraid. But if one was scared, they were welcome to leave. I often think about the one who leaves the army of God. They likely have not spent their time in the prayer closet, in solitude with God, or have an understanding of his word. The wisdom has not been received, nor has faith grown and produced fruit. Often, it is those full of themselves or caught up in the world's affairs. The cares and worries within one's life reside within one's inner being, just like the box I spoke about in the beginning.

2 Timothy 2:3-4 says, "Persevere for God with a soldier's attitude. You, therefore must endure hardship as a good soldier of Yeshua the Messiah. No one engaged in warfare entangles himself with the affairs of this life that he may please him who enlisted him as a soldier." Mark 4:19 says, "The worries of this life, the deceitfulness of wealth, and the desires for other things come in and choke the word, making it unfruitful." The fruit we produce comes from the spirit of God and training in upright living as a soldier. The distracted soldier bought tickets for the cruise ship, which is the world. While the trained soldier enlisted in the army of God, stepping on the battleship. The battleship is not always comfortable, but it's the greatest reward one can ever have.

We rarely see videos of people's heart's softened with eyes of tears, watching someone vlogging or advertising for a cruise ship. Instead, it provokes the worldly part of one's heart and mind, often lust, jealousy, and envy, with a longing to satisfy something within. But when we see a video of a retired veteran speaking about his experiences, in the end, we see the joy in his eyes, followed by a smile. It can bring even the most assertive individual to tears thinking about their sacrifice.

The battleship has greater contentment and eternal reward than the cruise ship. One who learns to weather the storm of life with God will sleep through the sea's waves. They can learn a lot by trusting in Yeshua and his words. Mark 4:38 says, "Yeshua was in the stern, sleeping on a cushion. The disciples woke him and said to him, "Teacher, don't you care if we drown?" Yeshua was at Peace in life's storms, but the disciples were not.

Luke 22:46, Yeshua said to his disciples, "Why are you sleeping?" he asked them. "Get up and pray so that you will not fall into temptation." When the storms raged in the outside world, Yeshua was at Peace and sleeping, but his disciples were in fear. However, Yeshua was not at Peace when the storm raged within himself. During this time, the disciples fell asleep and were too tired to pray.

It's easy for the flesh to fear when things from the outside world are out of our control, disturbed, and the waves are raging. Think about job loss, debt, physical illness, loss of a loved one, bankruptcy, foreclosure, repossessed car, or many other situations in life. The disciples wanted Jesus to save them in a physical circumstance with great fear all around them, where they were afraid to die. Concerning internal spiritual matters, they slept while Yeshua prayed and sweated blood in deep anguish. He was about to be put to death. By saying, "You will not die," Peter lacked faith, and Yeshua rebuked him.

Think about your life. We can often believe God is sleeping on us during our troubles in the world. We see all his disciples fell into temptation when they scattered from him at his crucifixion out of fear and faithlessness. How much more can we today separate from God when it comes to dying more to our flesh? Or how often can we lack prayer and trust in God when the boat gets rocked? They lacked faith. John 20:25, the disciples said, "Unless I see the nail marks in his hands and put my finger where the nails were, and put my hand into his side, I will not believe." Peter and Judas are also good examples of this lack of faith. Peter denied Yeshua three times, while Judas betrayed him for money.

God was still merciful with both of them. You might be feeling right now like you have betrayed or denied Jesus. Though you may have, God's hand is not too short that he can't forgive you.

Judas could not forgive himself, nor would he accept God's forgiveness. As a result, he hung himself on a tree due to the most significant distress and pain he felt inside. On the other hand, Peter could forgive himself and accept God's forgiveness. As a result, God used him mightily for his kingdom and throughout the rest of his life. Jesus also acknowledged how much he loved Peter, even after he denied him. No matter what, prayer is the most important thing we can do now and forever.

Yeshua is evident in Luke 21:36 "Be always on the watch, and pray that you may be able to escape all that is about to happen and that you may be able to stand before the Son of Man." We want to stand like Stephen while being stoned by the world. Standing with such confidence and faith in Jesus that you look up and see Jesus standing at the right hand of God in heaven. He was not sitting at the right hand but standing in amazement at Stephen's actions and courage.

As Romans 8:18 says, "For I consider that the sufferings of this present time are not worth comparing with the glory that is to be revealed to us."

Let us endure until the end, without wavering and without fear. Let one be of good courage and strength, with all the hope and perseverance of Yeshua the Messiah. He did not overcome the physical storms but the spiritual storms by being nailed to a cross as a criminal for our sins. Let us crucify our sins and flesh, and may our life be a blessing for God's kingdom and his eternal glory! Amen.

CHAPTER 6.

Is This the Dream

I remember being out on Anna Maria Island off the coast of Florida. I heard one of the most impactful words I have ever heard from someone in my lifetime. I was out on this island every morning before sunrise until sunset. As my usual daily routine began, I would pray to God while listening to the ocean waves crash—such a peaceful, serene environment on that beach without any other soul around. As the day grew bright and the sun rose over the horizon, I observed a man who caught my attention. He was a kind, humble, and respectful gentleman who liked picking up the trash after the others who'd left it behind. He often rinsed in the showers, sat at the picnic tables, prayed, rested, and read. I would give him canned goods and ask how his day was going. I knew there was something unique about this man from the moment I first saw him.

There was a light, a presence that followed him, and something that sparked my curiosity. This situation seldom occurred. Since I was young, my mother would tell me I reminded her of her mother. My grandmother could read people like an open book, an excellent discerner of character. God must have blessed me with this kind of discernment since birth.

As I observed this man, I felt a stirring in my heart that I must talk to him more and ask him questions. His words were so simplistic, yet one of the most powerful words ever to hit my ears.

He first began to tell me about his life in the military and later how he became a financial executive at a major firm. His wife had passed away, and he never remarried. He raised his children until they grew up and paid their way through college. He said once they moved out of the home, he sold it, gave the kids the vehicles, then donated to charity and gave them his assets. Then the most powerful words I have heard other than the gospel of Yeshua.

He mentioned how he believed he was living the dream but was still unhappy with his lifestyle. He spoke about the American dream and said these four words that hit me like a pound of bricks, "We are the dream." He pauses briefly to think while packing his bag on a bench near the showers and drying off in his swimming trunks. He looks at me and says, "Think about it." The words were so profound that I must have zoned out as if my body had become sucked into a black hole. Everything I ever knew became a black hole to me.

The words of Yeshua hit me strongly at that moment from 1 John 2:15-17. "Do not love the world or the things in the world. If anyone loves the world, the love of the Father is not in him. For all that is in the world, the lust of the flesh, the lust of the eyes, and the pride of life is not of the Father but is of the world. And the world is passing away, and the lust of it; but he who does the will of God abides forever." Those words have never left my heart, soul, or mind. In fact, since that time, God has consistently and fervently reminded me of those words. I was not just reading words from a page anymore. I saw a vision of those words in

3D, 8K, magnified in high definition. It struck me like lightning during a thunderstorm. It shook me to my core like an 8.0 earthquake at the top of a skyscraper. God spoke to me through that man.

Take a moment to think about those words. We are the dream building of Babylon's tower. We are the enslaved Israelites building the pyramids and a nation of many false gods. The American dream is the world's and people's dreams, as these three words speak for themselves. It's a dream. An illusion. A figment of one's imagination who believes this world is forever. One believes in their soul that what is today and tomorrow will be forever or have the hope that what is now will always be. Those see the temporary, but not eternity.

Many live within the box, like watching a fantasy Hollywood movie on a box-shaped TV. They never see outside the box of reality or turn off the TV to see what is real around them. It's like those who believe there is a glass dome in the sky and the Earth is flat. They prove that they are living in a box while too busy shaking the snow globe that they're trapped inside. They never truly escape the snow globe's entrapment to touch the real snow. Neither will they step out of the box to look up and see what's outside the universe.

The world is like a box, and within the box is a snow globe which is one's body, intellect, subconscious, soul, heart, and mind contained within it. The snow globe is made by human hands in a factory and sold to whoever buys it. It's fake inside, often cheap, with a human-manufactured design. Likewise, people love to watch the snow globe, just like they do their fantasy boxed TV or phone. Unless one breaks free from it all, they will remain trapped inside.

The American and global dreams are also like a snow globe. It's cheap, fake, designed by humans, and sold for a price. All four of these aspects can happen within our souls. Whoever chases this dream will never wake up. It's like never waking up from a deep sleep until you have breathed your last breath and your soul has reached heaven or hell. This "American Dream" statement reminds me of Jeremiah 51:39, "In their excitement, I will set out a feast for them and make them drunk so that they shout with laughter then sleep forever and not awake," declares the Lord."

God is speaking of Babylon here. It is physical and spiritual. Babylon can be seen and felt with our five senses, but it can also live within our hearts, souls, and minds. Again, the box and the snow globe analogy. But who can see eternity and wake up from this daze? God is saying that while people are excited by their lusts and pleasures. They enjoy their feasts with laughter. They are living in sin, loving entertainment, making money, enjoying business, shopping, eating, drinking, and ignoring God. He will cause them to sleep in the delusion and never wake again until their souls become cast away forever, where the flames never stop, and water and oceans don't exist. What dream is there outside of this world? What desiring plans exist when your body perishes, your heart stops, and your brain no longer connects with neurons?

We all know what dreaming is like after each night. Then we wake up, think about the dream, and sometimes ruminate about its meaning. How much more should we reflect on eternity and God's kingdom? Eternity is not a dream; it's reality. While the world is imaginary, destined for doom.

God says that those who reject him and live in willful sin will live under a strong delusion to believe a lie and what is false. 2 Thessalonians 2:10-12 clearly defines those who delight in wickedness rather than the truth of God's word.

Returning to the thought of that man on the beach, he left the world's dream to be content in the reality of God's kingdom. There is nothing wrong with owning a home or possessions. We read that

Abraham brought some of his possessions when he left his father's house to dwell in tents. But the truth is, even Abraham did not delight in holding onto the world. He did not put his tent pegs down and say, "This is my home!" Nor did he say, "I won't leave my mansion with over ten rooms or leave my mother and father." He left because he trusted a greater promise. Hebrews 11:8,10 says, "By faith Abraham obeyed when he was called to go out to a place he was to receive as an inheritance. He went out, wondering where he was going. "For he was waiting for the city that has foundations, whose architect and builder is God." Abraham was looking for something other than permanent dwellings on Earth with an attachment to the world. He saw eternity and dwelled in a temporary tent until he knew God intimately before arriving at heaven's gates.

The man I met on the beach didn't have to give up all those things to be declared righteous by God. Instead, he wanted a more intimate encounter and connection with God. He felt he had lost himself in the world, trapped inside a box and shaken in a snow globe. He smashed the snow globe within and crushed the box to be free. He saw a life of eternity with God and lost all attachment to the temporary. This man understood what was missing inside! He awoke from his dream and discovered the eternal reality he had longed for.

The world to him became like eating rotten eggs. It not only tasted bad, but it upset his stomach and made him sick inside. It's rare to meet someone who has truly awakened to the world around them, who is sick inside by the flavor of the world. If you also feel this way, you are usually labeled with a mental illness and avoided by society. On the other hand, those trapped inside trying to escape this life often consume themselves with drugs, sex, or alcohol instead of turning to God.

God is one's escape and freedom. God is one's rescuer and savior. He can smash the snow globe and destroy the box. God will give you a vision for the future without beginning and end, without walls or borders except for the boundaries of his kingdom.

Everything I am discussing here reminds me of a movie I saw many years ago called Cast Away. The film is about a man who was shipwrecked by a man-made boat. At first, he was fine. He was not lonely at all. As time went on, he started to become discontent. Psychosis began to kick in, and he gave a name to a volleyball, which became as valuable to him as human life. Wilson was his best friend. Unfortunately, I never saw him pray to God or seek his face.

If we think about our lives, we can become discontent when cast away from the world. We can begin to seek fake people around us, false religions and beliefs, or unrealistic fleshly desires that rage within our souls like ocean waves. The temptations that once were gone might creep back in, and the world will pull us back and forth like a rope in a tug of war. The ship's anchor might weigh us down and drag us to the bottom of the sea floor within the depths of our flesh. We might become bored, lonely, or unsettled within our souls. Finding peace in a place where we were once at rest beside the ocean waves has now become our greatest struggle.

One who doesn't find peace with God and be content alone with him must create another reality that wars against the soul. The mind and heart will war against the soul. If the flesh overcomes the soul, one will become delusional, and psychosis will occur. We then create a fairytale or imaginary lifestyle to appease our flesh, like the volleyball named Wilson in Cast Away. When in fact, we are Cast Away from God on a deserted island called Earth. Wouldn't being on an island with God rather than Cast Away from his presence be much more delightful and peaceful?

Imagine a tropical island in your mind for a moment. Envision an island in the middle of the sea, thousands of miles from anyone and far away from land. Picture a house on your island. You have abundant food, palm trees surrounding you, a Bible in your hand, and a white sandy beach in front of you. You can feel the warm breeze, smell the salt in the wind, and hear the wind blowing in your ears with the rustling of the palm branches. As you visualize a peaceful tropical paradise, be there with God. Could you remain in that place for eternity?

Now imagine what heaven might be like. Jesus said, "I will go and prepare a place for you." Then think about the trillions of galaxies in our solar system. Some people are focused on a small plot of land on Earth as if that's heaven now, but they don't think about owning 6 to 50 galaxies with even more fantastic sights than anyone could ever imagine. Look here in 1 Corinthians 2:9 "It is written, "What no eye has seen, what no ear has heard, and what no human mind has conceived" the things God has prepared for those who love him." Think about that momentarily. No one has imagined, seen, or heard what it would be like in his kingdom. It will be even more incredible than the galaxies or anything fathomable in this universe. I don't believe all of NASA and its space explorations, Hubble telescopes, or technology can even grasp a crumb from a slice of bread what God has prepared for those who love him. If God designed you to enjoy a specific environment in nature on Earth the most, imagine what he has prepared for you in eternity. If God did it initially with one man named Adam, best believe God means it when he says, "I will go and prepare a place for you."

God is a promise keeper! As long as you see the rainbow in the sky, keep that as a reminder that his promise is valid. The entire Earth has never flooded since his pledge. God also promised that no man will ever be able to snatch you out of his hand for all who repent and believe. Keep the faith, and continue running the race. Rest with God upon the island within your soul while praying to remain in his presence. Remember Psalm 51? "Cast me not away from your presence, oh Lord. Take not your holy spirit from me." We sing to God to remain in his presence, to walk in his ways, and to live a life of faith. We don't want the presence of God to bring fear, loneliness, guilt, or shame upon our lives like Adam and Eve, who sinned. We don't want to lose hearing God's voice or hide from him when he's calling our names, saying, "Where are you?"

A garden is a place of rest, and so is the island you envisioned with God. Don't let it become a place of being Cast Away. Adam and Eve were cast away from the Garden of Eden. Let your body and soul become the restored Garden of Eden.

In the temple of God in the holy of holies, God's spirit would hover over the Ark of the Covenant. In that Ark were the commandments of God, the manna, Aarons's budded rod, gold overlaying the Ark, and God's spirit hovering over the cherubim angels. The Ark symbolizes a new restoration or beginnings like Noah's Ark. The commandments are to be written on our hearts and minds by the holy spirit, as it's written in the new covenant in Ezekiel 36:26-27, Jeremiah 31:33, and Hebrews 10:16. Aarons Budded Rod symbolizes always being fruitful and bearing fruit. At the same time, the manna represents the bread of life, which is Yeshua. The gold on the Ark symbolizes becoming pure.

For example, gold in the ground must be purified and poured through a refining fire. As it's in the burning flames and melts the gold down, it brings out the impurities so that after someone has removed the gold from the flame, it will be pure solid gold. As 1 Peter 1:7 says, "These trials are so that the true metal of your faith (far more valuable than gold, which perishes though refined by fire) may come to light in praise and glory and honor at the revelation of Messiah Yeshua" As it's written in Zechariah 13:9 "This third I will put into the fire; I will refine them like silver and test them like gold. They will call on my name, and I will answer them; I will say, 'They are my people,' and they will say, 'The Lord is our God." God will test us in this life to see if our faith is pure and sincere.

Jeremiah 3:16 says that they will make no mention of the Ark anymore. The Ark of the Covenant is within us, as is his holy spirit dwelling within the soul. As 1 Corinthians 3:16 says, "Don't you know that you yourselves are God's temple and that God's Spirit dwells in your midst?" If we are not holy, how can we be the temple of God, where his spirit dwells? In Ezekiel 10, the spirit of God departed from the temple because of the continuous sinful acts of the people. Is it possible for God's presence to reside with someone who continually engages in a sinful lifestyle? No, it is not. In 1 John 3:6, it is clear that those who make a lifestyle of sinning have never seen God or known him. They may have had a spiritual and emotional experience, but without faith from hearing the word of God and repentance, how can one be made holy by the blood of the lamb and washed clean?

The priest would sprinkle the lamb's blood on the Ark of the Covenant. The horns on the four corners of the altar also had to be sprinkled with the blood of the lamb for the sacrifice to become accepted by God. If you look at the symbolism of the horns, it means the four corners of Earth and strength. In 1 Kings 12:26–33, Jeroboam and the people sinned by worshipping the golden calf with idolatry in Bethel and Dan. God warned through a prophet in Amos 3:14 that the altar's horns would become cut to the ground. These horns symbolize spiritual power and that God would cut them off and let them become destroyed.

Colossians 3:5 puts idolatry in a deeper perspective, "Therefore, put to death what is earthly in you. Sexual immorality, impurity, lust, evil desire, and greed for that is idolatry." We can't strengthen our salvation without the sacrifice of Yeshua, who cleanses idolatry and sin. In the temple, the priests would use specific instruments for service to God that were useful in serving him. Romans 6:13 reads, "Do not offer any part of yourself to sin as an instrument of wickedness, but rather offer yourselves to God as those who have been brought from death to life; and offer every part of yourself to him as an instrument of righteousness." How much more should we heed those words to be a valuable instrument for his temple service, which is your body? Romans 12:1 says, "Therefore, I urge you, brothers and sisters, in view of God's mercy, to offer your bodies as a living sacrifice, holy and pleasing to God. This is your true and proper worship." God is telling us how to worship him and what is pleasing to him. As Ephesians 5:1-2 says, "Therefore be imitators of God, as beloved children. And walk in love, as Christ loved us and gave himself up for us, a fragrant offering and sacrifice to God."

I like to reflect on the life of Solomon, who is a perfect example of living for the world and God. Solomon was known as the wealthiest man in history. Historians estimate that he earned between $40 to $58 billion annually from gold alone, not to mention his other business ventures. During one visit, the queen of Sheba gifted him with 22,644 kilograms or 49,921 pounds of gold. Overall, his net worth is estimated to be over $2.1 trillion in modern times. Sharing these details helps us understand the lifestyle he lived.

Solomon experienced and chased after everything in the world imaginable to man. He lived a life many living for the world could only dream of living. Solomon experienced all physical and sensual pleasures. He had more money than one could fathom. He had sex with over 1,000 women. He chased after every false God and idol to worship. He had all the fame, praises of men, and power in the world. He owned a mansion called a palace that took 13 years to build. It was massive, sitting at 150 feet long, 75 feet wide, and 45 feet high, as described in 1 Kings 7:1-25. When added together, his house was approximately 11,250sq/ft, not including the high ceilings. At the end of the day, what conclusion did Solomon come to? Ecclesiastes 1:14, "I have seen all the works that are done under the sun; and indeed, all is vanity and grasping for the wind." He called it meaningless and chasing after the wind!

Do you see how a life without living for God brings one down to the grave within one's body, mind, and soul? This verse confirms God's righteousness and highlights that the world's ways are not aligned with God's. Ecclesiastes 12:13 says, "Let us hear the conclusion of the whole matter: Fear God, and keep his commandments: for this is the whole duty of man." At the end of his life, Solomon realized that living for God and enjoying food was the only purpose of a man's life. He spoke about being content with working with your hands and living for God.

I look around the world today, regardless of the many countries I've traveled to, and I can't help but notice that many older men or women haven't grasped this profound reality of life. Elderly with kids grown and moved out are still trying to buy the largest homes and most expensive cars and striving to make more money. Many women frequently engage in beauty practices such as getting their hair styled, applying French-style nail polish, and using makeup and face creams in an attempt to maintain a youthful appearance. When will one wake up and smell the roses, realizing the rose will fade away and lose its color?

The scent we emit will eventually disappear, much like a flower cut from its stem in this world. We look beautiful for a time and might be pleasant to the eyes with our possessions, looks, and lifestyle. In time, it will all fade away and become replaced by the beauty of a gravestone above our heads in the ground.

The world's future may seem bleak, but it becomes bright when one lives for God. I'm not judging these individuals based on their lifestyle because it's possible for someone to genuinely love God with all their belongings and being. Instead, I'm giving an example, like the man at the beach who realized that the dream he was living was an illusion. He became aware that he was emerging from the dream where he lived in a world consumed by materialistic cravings and ambitions. He began to see eternity in his late 50s. His life was fading like a rose, drawing closer to being laid on the grave.

As Solomon wrote in Ecclesiastes 12:14, "God will bring every deed into judgment, including every hidden thing, whether it is good or evil." As Peter wrote in 1 Peter 4:7, "The end of all things is at hand; therefore, be self-controlled and sober-minded for the sake of your prayers." When someone cannot comprehend the concept of eternity, it can be compared to the feeling of wonder when looking out from the top of skyscrapers like the Burj Khalifa, World Trade Center, or Sears Tower. When someone does understand the concept of eternity, they start seeing life from a new perspective. It's like looking out the window of Noah's Ark and realizing that everything on Earth will eventually be destroyed, except for those who have prepared their souls like an Ark to weather the storm.

Our scent to God can either be pleasing or repulsive. Living for God can be compared to a romantic honeymoon after a wedding. The bride and groom will do their best to look fresh and well-groomed on their big day. They will likely bathe, wear nice clothes, and apply cologne or perfume to smell good. If someone lives a life of sin, it's like not showering for days and forgetting to wear deodorant while working out at the gym. They smell like body odor and are unpleasant for those in their vicinity.

Consider how our actions in this life might be perceived by God. Ephesians 5:1-2 "Therefore be imitators of God, as dearly loved children; and walk in love, just as Messiah also loved us and gave Himself up for us as an offering and sacrifice to God for a fragrant aroma." We should always strive to please God and never lose heart in living for Him. In the temple, people burned incense and spices as an offering to God. I experienced the delightful scent of both during my time in Israel. Imagine how wonderful our lives would be if our inner selves were fragrant with obedience and love for God and our fellow human beings.

I understand that Ecclesiastes may be challenging for individuals too focused on material possessions and worldly desires. However, if we shift our perspective to focus on eternity and hold onto the teachings of Yeshua, it can become easier to understand. We will begin to understand what John wrote in 1 John 2:17, "the world is passing away along with its desires, but whoever does the will of God abides forever." As previously stated, loving both the world and God is impossible. As individuals, we can dedicate ourselves to working hard, providing for our loved ones, and nurturing our spiritual well-being by constructing a temple within our soul, similar to the one in Jerusalem. Our goal is to create a welcoming environment filled with love, peace, and joy for everyone who enters. We aim to avoid the presence of money changers, pride, and business-minded individuals who prevent those seeking to worship and praise God. Our temple is dedicated to being a holy place where we prioritize loving God and our neighbors over money, self-interest, and lack of compassion. When a temple is used for selfish purposes, it becomes unfruitful, like the fig tree that Yeshua cursed.

Abel presented God with a flawless lamb as a gift from his heart filled with love and faith, while Cain gave crops from his field. Abel offered his best with his heart, soul, and mind, but Cain's offering of ordinary crops lacked genuine sincerity. God weighs and evaluates the motivations and intentions of the heart in everything we do. A person may travel around the world and do many good things in the name of God, but in the end, they may still be rejected by God at the judgment seat, despite their efforts. They may ask, "Lord, didn't I do all of this for you? Look at everything I accomplished!" Did we live and sacrifice by faith like Abel in Hebrews 11:4? What did you do with the grace that God has given you? Has it produced more fruits to become like him?

Many live loudly like a shofar or a cymbal, but how many are like a peaceful fruit, nourishing those who pick from the tree? Who is like David's heart in Psalm 23:1-2? "Adonai is my shepherd; I shall not want. He makes me lie down in green pastures. He leads me beside still waters.

He restores my soul. He guides me in paths of righteousness for His Name's sake." I think the man at the beach understood this verse well. It means that anyone can give up their worldly lifestyle, but they should always ask themselves if their actions are based on their faith. Many people are homeless, but some of them may not have faith. Many individuals have forsaken various things, but they have not found faith.

Additionally, many have made significant sacrifices but have been estranged from God's presence. The crucial issue is not the extent to which you are prepared to relinquish things but the intensity of your love for God. Take a moment to reflect on that island and imagine finding peace with God. Will you continue to seek his presence or succumb to fear like in the movie Cast Away? Your proper stance in eternity will be revealed when you discover it from within.

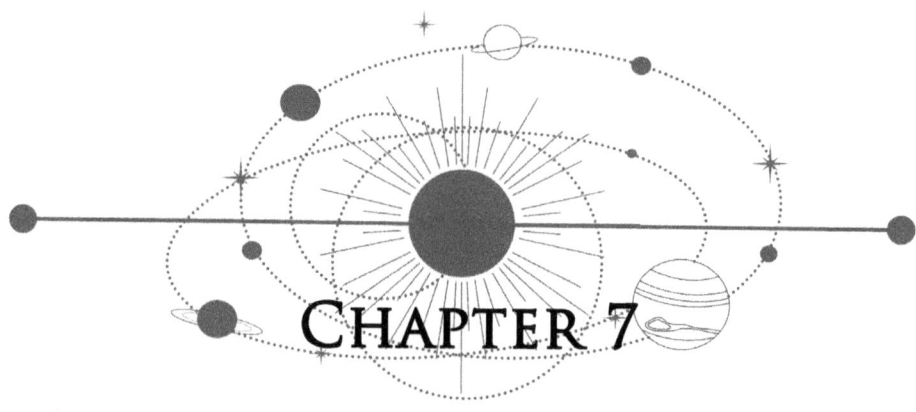

CHAPTER 7

The Blind and Eyes Seeing

I remember being in a room with a wealthy celebrity who had a way of making people laugh and feel captivated by his words. Even if he said something mundane, everyone around him would burst into laughter and look at him with admiration. I often contemplate how individuals perceive those with high financial or social status, but some may become uninterested during church services regarding God. In society, people frequently praise each other for accomplishments such as job promotions, graduating, acquiring new homes, cars, and pay raises. Do we receive enough praise for following God's teachings, living a virtuous life, and adhering to His values? It's common to spot signs, banners, or flags that read "Congratulations to my graduate" in someone's yard or on their house every year. When people graduate from high school or college, they often display their names on signs. I once saw a banner on a porch in Salt Lake City, Utah, from someone in the LDS Mormon church congratulating their son for becoming a missionary. However, Christians and Jews don't often congratulate or compliment each other for following a righteous path with God.

Picture a society where doing God's work is held in higher regard than being a celebrity, wealthy, social media influencer, politician, or influential individual. In such a society, the moral well-being of families and individuals would improve rather than decline. When considering our life, it is crucial to prioritize pleasing God and seeking His approval over the approval of others. Our ultimate goal should be to graduate with the seal of God upon us, much like a seal on a college diploma. Someone can excel in their profession without having much knowledge about the Bible. Similarly, they may be well-versed in sports players' names and statistics but unfamiliar with the Bible's content. While it's not our place to judge others, it's essential to identify a set of values and prioritize the five most significant ones for ourselves, striving to embody them in our daily lives. You will find inner prosperity by following those five core values and maintaining a devotion to God while striving to love and serve others. No matter what challenges life presents, you will remain content and undisturbed.

While it may feel good to receive compliments and praise from others, it's important to remember that true fulfillment comes from receiving praise from God and focusing on eternal values. The soul that seeks only temporary pleasure constantly searches for fleeting emotions, relying on external validation from those around them, unable to put their trust in God. In contrast, the prophets in the Bible lived a solitary life, but they never felt alone. They trusted in God, not in the world or others around them. God gave them a helper. They remained focused on completing the mission that God had given them. Their faith in God was unwavering.

Life's journey can be compared to a desert, where one may face spiritual challenges. Food and water are scarce in the desert, with extreme heat and tests one must endure. As life becomes tough and the heat of challenges beats down on us, we may feel like our flesh is burning. It can feel like we are in a desert, lacking the sustenance we need to thrive. When we lack the living water and bread of life, we will struggle to feel God's presence and guidance. That is the desert of testing along with the journey in the wilderness.

I think about when the devil tried tempting Jesus in the desert while he fasted for forty days and forty nights in the wilderness. Similar to Moses fasting for forty days and nights. The devil tempted Jesus with offers of pride, instant pleasure, healing, power, fame, and money. He tells him in Matthew 4:8, "All these I will give you if you will fall down and worship me." The devil was referring to everything that Jesus could ever imagine or desire, along with the kingdom of the world. If only Yeshua would bow down and worship him by worldly passions and desires. He might have received the praises of men from a worldly perspective, but by resisting the devil and keeping God's word, he completed God's mission. He received the greatest praise, worship, and glory alone. No wonder the devil is mad when you worship and praise God, obey him, and walk in his ways. He's jealous and wants to lead, be the center of attention, and be honored by men. How many still desire the praises of men now, seeing it from that perspective?

Jesus knew the devil was twisting the words in Deuteronomy to try and cause him to sin because the Holy Spirit was alive in him. Each time, Yeshua's response was always to worship God and him alone. How often, when you're down, going through struggles in life, feeling distant from God, or feeling far apart from him, can you hear a Bible verse in your head and then begin to doubt or have fear? That is how the devil spoke to Jesus in the wilderness. He caused depression and feelings of worthlessness in the prophets. He has even led some to commit suicide or turn back to sin. His intelligence allows him to manipulate and exploit our weaknesses and strengths. His ultimate goal is to weaken the strong wall and penetrate the weak. The closer you get to the sun, or in better terms, "the Son," the more your flesh will be burnt off. It leaves less of our flesh for the devil to touch. James 4:7 says, "Submit yourselves, then, to God. Resist the devil, and he will flee from you." As written in Galatians 5:16, "I say, walk by the Spirit, and you will not gratify the desires of the flesh."

As we return to the thought of the garden again, in Matthew 26:41, "Watch and pray so that you will not fall into temptation. The Spirit is willing, but the flesh is weak." The garden presented testing and temptations. While the Spirit may be willing, the flesh is weak. It's important to avoid overconfidence and not assume you won't stumble. As Proverbs 16:18 says, "Pride goes before destruction, a haughty spirit before a fall." Paul writes in 1 Corinthians 10:12, "If you think you are standing firm, be careful that you don't fall!" As humans, we all tend towards sin and weakness, but we aspire to be strong in the Spirit. Being prideful and believing we are already strong is like someone who overestimates their lifting ability at the gym and injures themselves. Similarly, we may think we are strong in our relationship with God, but we can still struggle with sin and weakness.

It's essential to exercise regularly and build muscle if you want to become stronger. As we create strength, we gain the ability to lift heavier weights. In the same way, we must grow spiritually with God in his gym to lift the weight of sin. Our relationship with God will become more solid when our spiritual muscles grow.

I found myself sitting and gazing out of the back window of a house one day. I spotted two trees: one evergreen and the other without leaves. A fence divided them. Days before, I observed birds frolicking in the evergreen tree - tweeting, singing, hopping, and interacting with each other. Although a bird occasionally perched on the leafless tree, it always appeared lifeless and dull. Two birds on the nearby fence were actively cleaning and preening themselves, seemingly oblivious to their surroundings. God taught me a valuable life lesson while sitting in a chair like an elderly gentleman, watching the trees and birds. A life filled with God is like the evergreen tree with happy birds, symbolizing fruitfulness, love, joy, and peace.

The bare tree with the unhappy bird represented a life without God, unfruitful, filled with worldly existence and sin. The birds on the man-made fence only cared for themselves, much like people trying to live for God and earthly and material things. Most people currently sit in comfort on the edge of the fence. They want to live with one hand embracing their worldly life and pleasures while the other hand is striving to cling to God.

I remember a phrase my mother used to say. "If candy is your weakness and you are overweight, don't go shopping down the candy aisle." She often talked about the concepts of right and wrong. It's best to avoid looking or walking toward the sin you struggle with most. You can't eat sugar candy while trying to lose weight on a diet. In the same way, you can't live in sin while trying to lose the weight of sin. I'm metaphorically speaking. If God blesses you with good health, it's essential to prioritize nutritious fruits and vegetables over processed and unhealthy options like GMOs, fast food, and sweets. Your soul will thank you for taking care of your body.

I recall visiting the gym in the past and encountering an overweight man who spent an hour running on the treadmill while I worked out with weights. I greeted him frequently and inquired about his well-being. We finished our workout at the same time. I headed to the grocery store to buy a protein shake and noticed the same man from the gym had a cart of chips, cake, cookies, and soda. He was even eating one of the cookies while shopping. I empathized with the man's internal struggles and offered encouragement whenever I saw him at the gym. I'd encourage him to keep going and how it was really good to see him. As our conversation continued, he inquired about my eating habits and how I maintained my physical fitness. Over time, he began losing weight.

I liked talking with him more than listening to the loud and intense athletes on steroids and growth hormones during a strongman competition. From a spiritual perspective, you can observe that the man resorted to food for comfort during an inner battle. Likewise, individuals may turn to sinful behavior for temporary relief, but the burden of guilt will not dissipate. Burning the fat on the altar during a sacrifice was instructed by God for a reason. The fat is the sin that needs to be burned off. It feels like a burden and can be difficult to shed, similar to the burning flesh of a lamb on a brazen altar.

It's vital to avoid consuming things that make us spiritually fat. Adhering to God's exercise and diet plan is important to achieve spiritual health. This plan focuses on keeping the heart, soul, and mind healthy for eternity. We cannot use artificial means to build spiritual muscle like steroids and HGH. We should solely rely on the word of God and the Holy Spirit. Guidance from God can help us lose body fat, while the Holy Spirit can assist in building muscle and maintaining a healthy diet. Galatians 5:22-23 is the diet and exercise plan we all need. "But the fruit of the Spirit is love, joy, peace, forbearance, kindness, goodness, faithfulness, gentleness and self-control. Against such things, there is no law." In addition, Matthew 5 provides instructions on what qualities God desires in a spouse or workout partner. God is the ultimate personal trainer if we yield to him and follow his routines and methods of healthy living. The world leads to spiritual unhealthiness, but following God's path can bring eternal benefits. As you read up to this point, you may wonder what actions you should take to complete God's work.

John 6:27-29 "Do not work for food that spoils, but for food that endures to eternal life, which the Son of Man will give you. For on him, God the Father has placed his seal of approval." Then they asked him, "What must we do to do the works God requires?" Yeshua answered, "The work of God is this: to believe in the one he has sent."

God simply asks us to have faith in Jesus and not to toil for perishable food. It's a straightforward request, unlike Elon Musk's complex mission of reaching Mars. Although many praise him, he lives in a temporary box within one galaxy. He has not yet uncovered the mysteries of God and the universe within himself, let alone those that exist beyond the boundaries of our observable universe. God encourages us to think beyond what we can see and work towards food that has eternal value. This requires thinking outside the box and expanding our perspective beyond the universe we can observe.

The one who sees outside the box and beyond the universe is the one which God says "work for food that endures to eternal life." According to God, he approves of these and has placed his mark of approval on them. In the book of Revelation, the same seal is put on the righteous and believers in Jesus. How much more should we be encouraged not to let our hearts and minds become set on the temporary world? How much more should we become focused way beyond the traceable universe? How much more should we look beyond the limitations of our flesh and live by the Holy Spirit with all its ability to perform signs, miracles, and wonders? Matthew 17:20 says that one can move mountains with faith as small as a mustard seed. That's whole kingdoms, nations, and people.

I remember being in a dark and empty forest at night, with no lights or buildings for miles. The only source of light was a tiny penny-sized light held by the person I was with. That small device gave off a powerful beam of light that lit up the forest and all the little animal eyes nearby. Like a mustard seed, even the most minor light can dispel darkness and draw attention, much like the animals in that darkness.

This brings back memories of my mission trip to Israel. One evening, we had just finished having dinner. I was driving the vehicle alongside the western side of the Sea of Galilee with two others. I am an excellent driver, but remember how I mentioned before not to think you won't stumble? This one particular night, while driving through a roundabout, I accidentally hit a curb which caused one of my tires to burst. A gate guard to a small community sat staring at us and the vehicle, which had now stopped. We got out and began changing the tire with complete silence all around us as we laughed and joked with one another. I noticed a big hill in the dark near the spot where we had a flat tire. Then the words of Yeshua spoke to me from Matthew 5:14-16. "You are the light of the world. A town built on a hill cannot be hidden. Neither do people light a lamp and put it under a bowl. Instead, they put it on its stand, and it gives light to everyone in the house. In the same way, let your light shine before others, that they may see your good deeds and glorify your Father in heaven." We experienced a flat tire in the middle of the night while driving on a hill where Yeshua spoke about becoming the world's light.

It is important to let your light shine in any circumstance so others can see God. Let us shine as a beacon of light in a world that lacks the enlightenment of Christ. We should not allow a flat tire or the surrounding darkness to deter us from our mission. We are a light on a hill shining for the world to see. We let our good deeds light the way so others might praise and glorify God's name. You could be the only source of hope for someone, just like Yeshua often reached out to one individual. In a world filled with darkness and despair, that single light was the only glimmer of hope they had ever witnessed.

One who lives for the world has no hope; their future has no certainty. But one who lives for God has hope and a future, knowing their eternal destiny. It is written in John 5:24, "Truly, truly, I say to you, whoever hears my word and believes him who sent me has eternal life. He does not come into judgment but has passed from death to life." You will not go before the judge for the crimes and sins you have committed on earth. You will become exonerated and free of charges without an eternal prison sentence. All because of the sacrifice of Yeshua, who paid your debts and freed you from the death penalty. The judge is God, but those who do not believe and repent of their sins will not have dismissal for their crimes. When you die, you will have no second chances, tribunals, or bail bonds. You have a choice between graduating to either heaven or hell. You can decide which eternal career and environment you want to participate in. Whether peace and rest for eternal life or terror, fear, and fighting against flames for eternal life.

In Matthew 11:30, Yeshua says, "For my yoke is easy, and my burden is light." His labor on earth is easy, and his burden is light. He will not weigh you down like a 1000-lb weight in the gym. He aims to relieve you of your burdensome load of 1000 pounds and replace it with a lightweight one-pound weight.

In Acts 16:30-31, the prison guard asks Paul, "What must I do to be saved?" Paul replies, "Believe in the Lord Jesus, and you will be saved you and your household." We can sometimes overcomplicate the gospel and how we should live for God. God's truth is straightforward, but humans complicate it and make it difficult. Living a life devoted to God is not a difficult task in itself. However, the constant distractions and conflicting influences from the world around us can make it challenging.

Consider the construction of the Roman Colosseum and the financial sources that contributed to its creation. When the Romans went to war against Jerusalem in 70 A.D., they took all of the gold and riches from Israel. The Colosseum was financed using the resources within the temple, including its artifacts. As a result, the Colosseum was an epicenter for entertainment, sports, games, and distraction for Christians and other religions alike.

1 Corinthians 6:19 says, our bodies are the temple of God. Consider how this relates to your perspective on living in the world and your relationship with God. Will you allow the world to steal your temple's

utensils, riches, and belongings? Will you let the world, like the Romans, tear down your walls and ransack the wealth of God within you?

The Coliseum was a place for killing believers and distracting people from revolting against the government. The same is here today. If they can keep you entertained by the Colosseum, called social media, T.V., video games, sports, and chasing money and striving after more, they are already killing Christians and believers in Yeshua. One's soul is spiritually being ripped apart by the lions and devoured by the teeth of the enemies while people cheer them on. Don't lay down your eternal treasures and crown of life when you can significantly serve the kingdom of God.

We know that the Temple in Jerusalem was destroyed by God's will due to the rejection of Yeshua. Yeshua said in Matthew 24:2, "Do you not see all these things? Truly I say to you, not *one* stone here will be left upon another, which will not be torn down." This prophecy, along with the grace of God, has enabled the gospel to reach the four corners of the earth.

I'm encouraging you to live your life with a purpose bought with the blood of Christ rather than purchased for use in the world. Devote more time to God for his temple service rather than utensils used for the world. There is a reason the utensils in the temple needed to be made holy and consecrated for dedicated use. God desires you to be holy and use you for glory and purpose. It's important to know that the priests laughed, sang, ate, drank, and enjoyed fun. Yet, they were not to sin and live like the sinful world.

In Matthew 6:30-32, we read that the worldly worried about what they would eat, drink, wear, and other worries of life. But Yeshua said that God knows that you need those things. Seek him and his kingdom first; the rest will be added unto you. That is the key that unlocks the door, seeking him and his kingdom first. Sports, your job, clothes, house, new car, food, shopping, entertainment, and money must never come before God. The desire to have God's presence must be stronger and more pleasurable than the desire for others' wants and needs. John 10:10 "The thief comes only to steal and kill and destroy; I came so that they would have life, and have it abundantly."

If God delivered you from Egypt, you must pass through the Red Sea and become cleansed. Look straight into eternity, don't wander to the left or the right, or you might drown. Keep the faith that he will be with you wherever you go, don't be discouraged or afraid, for God is your salvation and strength. Proverbs 4:25-27 "Let your eyes look directly ahead And let your gaze be fixed straight in front of you. Watch the path of your feet, And all your ways will become established. Do not turn to the right or the left; Turn your foot from evil."

CHAPTER 8

Who God Sees

While on a mission trip to a poverty-stricken region in South America, I encountered a girl who left a lasting impression on me. I came across a place where the buildings had plywood and aluminum roofing, and some of the walls were left uncovered, which had tarps draped over them. My team and I brought food to provide for multiple families living there. There was a young girl, around five years old, who reached out her hand for a small bag of rice. I handed it to her, and she clutched it tightly, hugging it like a teddy bear. She hugged me with a big smile filled with joy and gratitude afterward. This little girl had something unique about her, making me wonder if God views us in a similar way.

Through my missions and work for God, I have had the privilege of working with thousands of children. Some kids have a special way of speaking to my heart and tugging at my heartstrings more than others. I believe that God may use certain people more than others because they are a cleaner vessel for his holy water to be poured into. Besides, why would anyone put clean water in a dirty glass with mud and dirt?

Let's think about the life of Jacob, who had twelve sons, but his heart was particularly drawn to one son. Joseph was the one who tugged at his heartstrings the most. Genesis 37:3 says that Jacob loved him because he was the son of his old age, but why was this child different from the rest? God not only shared dreams with Joseph but also spoke directly to him. Although Joseph was the youngest, he was also the most humble and affectionate. Joseph's brothers were jealous and greedy and sold him into slavery, much like Judas did to Jesus. However, Joseph remained devoted to serving God with his whole being, even while working for the king of Egypt. Despite his difficult circumstances, God used Joseph in a great way. Joseph demonstrated his devotion to God by being a light in a world consumed by darkness. Despite facing temptation and false accusations from the Pharaoh's wife, he remained steadfast in his morals, values, and faithfulness to God. Joseph refused to worship any other gods and stayed true to his beliefs.

Do we resist temptation when we're alone? How often? Our true character is revealed in the darkness. Joseph was blessed with great wisdom, understanding, and discernment from God. He received prophecies and dreams and had the ability to interpret them. Joseph was not interested in being a leader or having control over others. This was evident when he was falsely accused and thrown into prison by the Pharaoh. Regardless, Joseph remained humble and devoted to God in his heart and mind. Even though Joseph had to endure tests in prison, God eventually used him when the Pharaoh had a troubling dream.

Even the most knowledgeable magicians and wise men could not grasp the meaning of Pharaoh's dream. Much like Nebuchadnezzar and his magicians could not decipher the writing on the wall. Fortune tellers, diviners, and enchanters were also unable to comprehend it. God says in 1 Corinthians 1:19, "I will destroy the wisdom of the wise; the intelligence of the intelligent I will frustrate." People who prioritize worldly matters may struggle to understand the present or make predictions about the future. They are confused and unstable in all of their ways. Similar to Joseph's brothers reacting with anger and ridiculing his prophetic dreams.

Yeshua told the Pharisees in Matthew 16:3, "You know how to interpret the appearance of the sky, but you cannot interpret the signs of the times." In the same way, those who live according to the ways of the world will experience a troubled mind, similar to that of Pharaoh. Deuteronomy 28:28 says, "The Lord will afflict you with madness, blindness, and confusion of mind." This message targets individuals who fail to love and adhere to God's commandments. It is reiterated in 2 Thessalonians 2:11, "For this reason God sends them a powerful delusion so that they will believe the lie." A delusion that can't understand what is true. 1 Kings 22:22 clearly shows this: "I will go out and be a deceiving spirit in the mouths of all his prophets,' he said. "'You will succeed in enticing him,' said the Lord. 'Go and do it."

In this context, men's hearts were hardened, the prophets were proud, and people followed their desires. They did not want to listen to the voice of God or the one true prophet telling them, "Do not go to war," but they didn't listen. As Romans 1:28 says, "Furthermore, just as they did not think it worthwhile to retain the knowledge of God, so God gave them over to a depraved mind, so that they do what ought not to be done." God allows those who choose not to follow, love, and obey him to be ruled by other spirits and the desires of the flesh. In the end, when the writing is on the wall, the dreams and times can't be interpreted or understood.

I have always preached that one can read the Bible 50,000 times, cover to cover and front to back, and still not know God or feel his presence. Who wants to draw closer to God and live for Him in order to gain knowledge and wisdom?

Many times in my life, I've heard people express their difficulty in understanding what they're reading. This includes individuals from various religions, such as Mormon LDS, Muslims, and Judaism. They must have man's interpretation with other additional writings that they deem more important than the Bible. The Book of Mormon, the Quran, and the Talmud all come from men who could not read the writing on the wall or interpret the dreams and visions of God. These diviners were too focused on chasing worldly desires to recognize the existence of God, who is the creator of all things.

I once heard a Mormon explain that some people find the new testament and the Bible too difficult to understand. According to their beliefs, God sent Jesus to America to gain a better understanding of the Bible. The truth is Joseph Smith had a hunger for power, greed, money, and sexual lust. Why do you think he had to write something different outside of the Word of God? His heart was not right. There was no connection to God or the presence of the Holy Spirit.

You see, people must seek help from others when there is confusion, no answer, or no relationship with God, like Pharaoh and Nebuchadnezzar. They need to ask other men for understanding, knowledge, and wisdom. The divine answer was given only to Joseph and Daniel, as they were the ones who were seeking and committed to God. James 3:7 says, "The wisdom that comes from heaven is, first of all, pure; then peace-loving, considerate, submissive, full of mercy and good fruit, impartial and sincere." Perhaps that is why some individuals tug at God's heartstrings more than others. He seeks those with similar hearts to this verse referenced from James.

If a religion has a leader or a missionary, they are expected to represent the religion. They are supposed to reflect the character of their beliefs and their spiritual and moral behavior. Why would they send someone opposite to their religion and beliefs? In the same way, why would God use a man or woman who has not conformed to his image?

As Romans 12:2 is clear, "Do not conform to the pattern of this world, but be transformed by the renewing of your mind. Then you can test and approve what God's will is his good, pleasing, and perfect will." To renew your mind daily, focus on Colossians 3:2. "Set your minds on things above, not earthly things." As Philippians 4:8 dives deeper, "Finally, brothers and sisters, whatever is true, whatever is noble, whatever is right, whatever is pure, whatever is lovely, whatever is admirable if anything is excellent or praiseworthy think about such things."

By aligning our souls with God's character, we can discern what is pure and pleasing to Him. We will clearly understand God's plan for our lives without relying on others to interpret it for us. When we focus on eternity by faith, life becomes easier to navigate. We can follow the example of Abraham, who held onto a hope for a better future. Can we also see a brighter future for ourselves?

As we reflect back to Joseph's life, we can see that he saved his nation and the surrounding nations from famine. He became the world's most outstanding leader by combining his exceptional project management skills with the wisdom of God. To determine Joseph's capacity for forgiveness, God tested him when his brothers visited Egypt in search of food during the famine. Romans 12:20 says, "If your enemy is hungry, feed him; if he is thirsty, give him something to drink. For by doing this, you will heap fiery coals of shame on his head." Joseph did this very thing with a heart of forgiveness in helping his brothers, his father, and the surrounding nations. By demonstrating God's love for his neighbor and utilizing his entrepreneurial skills, he brought honor to God through his character and business acumen. Pharaoh acknowledged God when he told Joseph, "Since God has informed you of all this, there is no one as discerning and wise as you are. You shall be in charge of my house, and all my people shall be obedient to you."

Are we glorifying God by utilizing the gifts bestowed upon us, such as wisdom, knowledge, and understanding, which originate from our hearts? Or are we getting support from other men? When things get overwhelming, can we turn to God's saving grace for help with our troubled minds? Matthew 5:16 encourages us to let our light shine before men so that God will receive glory and praise from others. It seems that those who receive God's grace, much like a child, are the ones who tug at God's heartstrings the most.

A little child is eager to learn, quick to forgive, and full of love and joy if raised healthy. As Matthew 18:3 says, "Yes! I tell you that unless you change and become like little children, you won't even enter the Kingdom of Heaven!" He says that the kingdom of heaven is given to those who have the qualities of little children. I am reminded here of the story of the girl who embraced the bag of rice as if it were a gift from Jesus for eternal life. It makes me think about how much more we should be filled with joy, love, and gratitude.

This ties into Matthew 13, "The kingdom of heaven is like treasure hidden in a field. When a man found it, he hid it again and then, in his joy, went and sold all he had and bought that field. "Again, the kingdom of heaven is like a merchant looking for fine pearls. When he found one of great value, he went away and sold everything he had and bought it." Remember the man at the beach I spoke of in the earlier chapter? After finding a valuable pearl and precious treasure, he let go of all worldly attachments. Living a life filled with love, humility, and devotion to God can profoundly impact the lives of others, the universe, and eternity.

In order to comprehend God's wisdom and knowledge, it is necessary to surrender our own will and recognize the worth of His everlasting kingdom. Joseph, David, Abraham, Isaac, Jacob, Amos, Moses, and Abel serve as examples of shepherds who have surrendered their own desires, valued God's kingdom, and glimpsed eternity. While tending to their flocks with humility, they would have spent ample time in God's presence. In ancient times, society deemed them to be of low importance, but the time spent with God was more valuable than any amount of money or praise from people.

I have a friend who has heard me preach in my sermons, "Go stare at trees. You will find more of God there than anywhere else." He took it literally by accepting a job caring for trees on a tree farm. While caring for the trees, he had all the time to spend with God, seek his presence, and learn much about who God is. Amos also found the presence of God while shepherding and taking care of trees, and God used him significantly for his glory. Amos 7:14 Amos answered Amaziah, "I was neither a prophet nor the son of a prophet, but I was a shepherd, and I also took care of sycamore-fig trees."

David also understood this in Psalm 1:1-3, "How blessed is the man who does not walk in the counsel of the wicked, Nor stand in the path of sinners, Nor sit in the seat of scoffers! But his delight is in the law of the Lord, And His law he meditates day and night. He will be like a tree firmly planted by streams of water, Which yields its fruit in its season And its leaf does not wither; And in whatever he does, he prospers." According to God, we are like a tree that finds joy in following his laws and stays away from those who are arrogant, sinners, or proud. Those who love God's laws and contemplate them day and night while marveling at His wonders and glory, he says we will bear fruit and become firmly rooted like a tree with peace beside still waters.

It is stated in the Bible that we will prosper in all aspects of our lives through our relationship with God rather than just in terms of career success or wealth. This refers to our journey of serving and living for Him. Amos found success in tending to his flock and nurturing trees during his time of isolation from the world and its distractions. Isolation and getting alone are something an individual in society rarely does. It is worth noting that many influential individuals in the Bible who were used powerfully by God often spent a significant amount of time alone.

If your life is full of loud events like concerts or sports games, will you be able to hear God speak to you? How can God communicate with you in a small, still whisper if you're racing around like cars on an interstate?

Let's tune out the noise and distractions of the news, social media, and TikToks and instead tune in to the serene, sweet melodies of the angels. We delight in listening to birds singing on a lovely spring morning. Let's simply find tranquility by being still like calm waters and watching the sun rise over a majestic mountain lake.

Yeshua emphasizes the significance of solitude in Matthew 6:6 by saying, "But when you pray, go into your room and shut the door and pray to your Father who is in secret. And your Father who sees in secret will reward you." He continues to say that those who pray in silence with a humble soul will receive blessings. Why would God tell us to go into our room and shut the door to pray?

Yeshua regularly prayed alone with God, as revealed in Mark 1:35. "Rising very early in the morning, while it was still dark, he departed and went out to a desolate place, and there he prayed." The conclusion here is God will provide rewards for individuals who maintain a quiet and humble spirit while pursuing a relationship with Him in isolation.

Yeshua teaches us not to show off our good deeds to others. Instead, we should be humble and keep them between ourselves and God. When he says, "Don't let your left hand know what your right hand is doing." He's commanding us not to be proud of our works and to avoid seeking validation from others when performing good deeds.

The need for validation from others may often be traced back to father-related issues during childhood. When a father is absent, it can lead to feelings of abandonment, feeling unheard, not being listened to, or rejection. Some individuals tend to constantly seek approval and validation from others, particularly regarding their successes, accomplishments, and achievements in life. Some might engage in acts of kindness and perform good deeds to feel validated by others and gain approval from God. On the contrary, God desires a humble, pure, and sincere heart filled with gentleness and love.

When Moses and Joshua climbed to the peak of Mount Sinai, Moses did not announce his accomplishments with a shofar or trumpet blast. They isolated themselves to listen to God's voice, and both sought solitude. People who refused to isolate themselves and be alone urged Aaron to create a golden calf. Aaron caved under peer pressure and sought validation from others by instructing and helping them build the golden calf. He prioritized pleasing others and earning their praise more than pleasing God.

Imagine if your favorite teacher, preacher, or church said, "I am disappearing to spend time with God." How many would get bored or lose patience and seek another teacher, preacher, or church? How many would assume he's sinful, dead, or suddenly developed a mental disorder? How many would say, like the Israelites, "We don't know what's come of him." Since they didn't seek God, stay patient, spend time alone, or maintain their faith, they had to devise their worship plan.

While the Israelites were living in Egypt, they would worship their gods with sexual immorality, gold and silver, and selfish desires. Exodus 32:4 says, "These are your gods, Israel, who brought you up out of Egypt." How could someone so quickly depart from the faith after seeing signs, wonders, miracles, and being delivered from Egypt? It's simple; they lacked trust and confidence in God. People today will become impatient and resort to worshiping money like gold and silver and sexual immorality such as sex out of marriage, pornography, and sinful living.

After spending forty days and forty nights away, Moses delayed his return. During this time, the Israelites indulged in worshipping and dancing around the golden calf. When Moses descended from the mountain, he witnessed the people standing defenseless and naked before their enemies. They did not keep their garments clean. They were not clothed in the garments of righteousness or waiting patiently like Moses on top of the mountain.

But as for us, Yeshua has washed our garments clean so we can stand before Him clothed in righteousness. We must wait patiently for Yeshua's return to the mountain, like Moses waiting on Mount Sinai.

Like the Israelites who witnessed God's deliverance from Egypt, many individuals today observe signs and wonders in the moon, stars, and weather. Those with biblical knowledge can recite verses about the end times and connect them to present-day events. However, it can be difficult for them to genuinely worship and give thanks to a holy God when they fail to prioritize moments of solitude devoted to Him. It's even more difficult without the fun programs, church bands, activities, entertainment, or life's attractions in general.

When an occurrence in life brings uncertainty, discomfort, abandonment, rejection, fleshly desire, or fear, they are more prone to being tempted to build the golden calf in the wilderness. Although one has seen deliverance in the past by melting the gold in flames, the testing will reveal whether it will be pure gold for God's kingdom or become a golden idol for the world. One with an idol heart and mind is like the Israelites telling Moses, "Give us more to eat and drink." The Israelites in the desert were always dissatisfied and discontent, constantly groaning and complaining due to a perceived lack of resources. What does God say again? Hebrews 13:5 "Keep your lives free from the love of money and be content with what you have, because God has said, "Never will I leave you; never will I forsake you."

Don't let material possessions and desires consume your life to the extent that you mold your idea of God to suit your personal preferences and lifestyle. If someone tries to manipulate and alter the concept of

God to match their desires, they will likely misunderstand His teachings and try to force them into their mold. You may find yourself surrounded by people who share your worldly mindset rather than following the word and laws of God with patience and reverence. It's crucial to seek out those with similar values and principles. The worship of the golden calf is meant for individuals who prioritize worldly possessions and have a short-sighted perspective. While Mount Sinai is for those with a long-term vision and focus on eternity.

After Moses came down from the mountain, his face radiated so bright that nobody could bear to look at him. After Yeshua descended from the transfiguration mountain, his face also glowed to the point where it was impossible to look directly at him. The glow symbolizes the presence of the Holy Spirit, divine holiness, and the glory of God.

Those filled with the Holy Spirit may cause those who operate in the flesh to feel uneasy. One's soul, filled with the Holy Spirit, cannot gaze upon the soul within. It's similar to how your eyes feel after sitting in a dark room for an hour and suddenly turning on bright lights that require you to cover your eyes. It is impossible for someone with darkness in their eyes to look at someone full of light. The radiant glow emanates from one's deep connection with God, gained through solitary contemplation and a profound understanding of His heart and love.

It is important to remember that God does not intend us to live in isolation forever or become arrogant in our pursuit of holiness and enlightenment. Even Moses, who was very righteous, remained humble and wore a veil to avoid flaunting his righteousness before men. He was careful not to make others feel inferior to him. After forty days and nights of isolation, Moses had to come down from the mountain. Similarly, Noah left the ark, Elijah left the cave, the high priest left the holy of holies, Samuel left the temple, and Abraham left his tent.

We all have a purpose in God's plan to be a shining light with a radiant face. Our inner light should not be hidden but shine for all to see. Didn't Thomas Edison invent the lightbulb with the intention of providing light for everyone to see? Likewise, Yeshua gave us his holy spirit as a light for all to see. Yeshua set a flawless example for us to follow in our daily lives. Luke 21:37-38 "Each day Jesus was teaching at the temple, and each evening he went out to spend the night on the hill called the Mount of Olives, and all the people came early in the morning to hear him at the temple."

Paul encouraged Timothy with the same lifestyle as we read in 2 Timothy 4:2, "Preach the word; be prepared in season and out of season; correct, rebuke and encourage with great patience and careful instruction. We can see that the life of Yeshua follows a similar pattern. He would pray, teach, correct, rebuke, and encourage with patience while carefully teaching others. He was restoring the connection that Adam and Eve had lost in the garden by spending time with God.

God desires for you to live a fulfilling and gratifying life by loving what he loves and hating what he hates. Psalm 16:1 says, "You make known to me the path of life; you will fill me with joy in your presence, with eternal pleasures at your right hand." Our responsibility is to discover and embrace the happiness, contentment, and enjoyment life offers. No human alive will ever find it in the world unless they live a rewarding life serving others, spreading the good news, teaching others God's ways, loving His commandments, and praying and spending time with Him.

Don't only memorize His words; try to fully absorb and understand them, like savoring your favorite meal. Jeremiah 15:16 "Your words were found, and I ate them, and your words became to me a joy and the delight of my heart, for I am called by your name, O Lord, God of hosts." Allow it to fill you inside like the bread of life and living water, as Yeshua referred to. John 6:35 "Then Yeshua declared, "I am the bread of life.

Whoever comes to me will never go hungry, and whoever believes in me will never be thirsty." Would you be willing to provide both physical and spiritual nourishment to others? As Matthew 25:35-40 says, "For I was hungry, and you gave me something to eat, I was thirsty, and you gave me something to drink, I was a stranger, and you invited me in, I needed clothes, and you clothed me, I was sick, and you looked after me, I was in prison, and you came to visit me."

Have you experienced true love and compassion within yourself? Has the patience and endurance of teaching God's word to one soul, like Philip with the Ethiopian, been brought to life with love? Who has spent time with the least of God's people while other men revel in their glory? Luke 15:10 "In the same way, I tell you, there is rejoicing in the presence of the angels of God over one sinner who repents." The joy that God and the angels experience when someone repents is far greater than any physical challenges that may arise when trying to reach that one soul.

I leave you with this thought in Psalm 5:11. "But let all who take refuge in you be glad; let them ever sing for joy. Spread your protection over them, that those who love your name may rejoice in you." Let us take refuge in him like the disciples at the Transfiguration mountain or like taking shelter in a house during a thunderstorm. Let us become transfigured into his likeness and glory. Let us find protection and peace in him like Moses on Mount Sinai. Those who seek shelter in God and love Him will experience joy and rejoice. Proverbs 18:10 "The name of the Lord is a strong tower; the righteous man runs into it and is safe."

Jeremiah 17:5-7 says, let us not trust in man or the flesh for strength, but rather the living God. And John 14:21 says, "He who has My commandments and keeps them is the one who loves Me. He who loves Me will be loved by My Father, and I will love him and reveal Myself to him." God can only reveal himself to us when we love him with all our hearts, soul, and mind—intimately loving his ways with gladness, joy, thankfulness, and a desire to humbly obey. 1 John 2:5 says, "Whoever keeps his word, in him truly the love of God is perfected. By this, we may know that we are in him." If we love his ways and keep them, the love of God has been made whole within us and the world God has cast out. 2 John 1:6 goes even further, saying to keep his commandments and to love, which you have heard from the beginning. He also tells us to love each other and God. Yeshua says that the laws and the prophets hang upon those two. Loving God and loving one another was in the garden before men sinned and began acting wickedly. God had to give more laws to bring us back to what is right. Then God gave us his Holy Spirit as a new covenant.

It's written in Galatians 3:24, "Therefore the Torah [Law] became our guardian to lead us to Messiah, so that we might be made right based on trusting." In the end, Yeshua said on the cross, "It is finished." All can be returned to the Tree of Life for eternity rather than the forbidden Tree of Death. Walk in the spirit, and you will not gratify the works of the flesh. Amen.

CHAPTER 9

What Do You See

I started encouraging others to look at their baby pictures to remember who they were before the world began influencing them. I took my advice and pulled out my own 9-month-old baby pictures. I took it even further and looked at my 2-year-old photos. We will begin to see what has been changed based on the effects of trauma, pain, hurt, and negative memories in your mind. We will also understand how TV, social media, music, school, and bad influences can infiltrate our minds and change our perspectives. When you have an older, unclean song replaying in your head or when you say certain popular trendy words or phrases. When you act and behave differently, such as participating in popular challenges like planking, the cinnamon challenge, the crate challenge, and modern dances, usually these are influences we pick up on from school and society. These influences can shape our attitudes, characters, thoughts, and actions from a young age. I observed that what is often in our eyes as a child is exactly how our eyes should look up to God. Let's continue to dive deeper beneath the surface of your internal ocean.

Recognizing and coping with past hurts can be difficult. Memories of divorce, physical abuse, emotional trauma, and neglect all stem from our experience of being hurt in the past. Because it can be hard to forgive and pray for someone who has hurt us, these hurts can lead to recurring challenges. If you were never told as a child, "Good job, I'm proud of you, you're smart, you are talented, you're handsome or beautiful," or even "I love you," how much would that affect your thoughts and personality as an adult? A child who has dealt with any kind of abuse or experienced divorced parents will often repeat the same matter in a relationship or marriage, or they will repeat the same actions as their parents. Likewise, if you grew up with an alcoholic parent who smoked or is addicted to porn, you would be more likely to repeat the same matter.

Why does this occur? Let's take neglect and rejection, for instance. If, throughout your childhood, your parents did not attend your sports games, plays, or music recitals or watched you do something that was important to you or took an interest in, you have likely felt rejection. You have felt neglected if you tried to express your feelings and emotions to your parents and communicate your thoughts but feel that no one is listening. As a result, neglect can lead to communication issues later in life, and rejection can lead to bitterness and unforgiveness that shape your character. If someone grows up with divorced parents, no matter how hard one tries to avoid it, statistics prove they will also be more prone to divorce themselves. Before the divorce occurs, they will unconsciously repeat the same matter as their parents.

If your parent loved money, had a porn issue, was an alcoholic, cheater, or just a lazy bum, the same matter and characteristics will likely repeat from you. It's less likely to recognize those patterns without seeking Christian Counseling or Psychotherapy from a licensed therapist while seeking an unchanging, long-suffering God. I've witnessed even the strongest Christians, Jews, and Messianic Jews marry but end up miserable or divorced. One must recognize the negative flaws within oneself before the world around them and within them changes. One must recognize the positive traits within oneself to become a better version of themself. God intends you to become like him, but layers inside the soul can become buried underneath like geology rocks that someone must uncover. Over the years, layers build on layers, but those layers of the worldly influence that harden us must be dug up and removed to find the treasure within your soul. When you find the treasure, you can value God's prize that he sees in you.

God intends you to be like a child sitting on his lap. How would you behave on his lap? How would you act in front of God or around other children? Would you love others around you? Would you be quick to forgive? Would you be compassionate and gentle? Would you be jealous? Many are God's children among us, but do we see them as such?

When we are hurt, we associate our previous wounds and scars with those who inflicted them upon us. Although someone may cause a bruise or reopen old wounds, we must dig beneath the surfaces of our earth to get to the core. God desires to bring healing into your life and heal those scars, bruises, and wounds.

As we look back on the Garden of Eden, it took two people to sin, which brought guilt, shame, and harm into their lives. It will also take two people to bring healing to one's life. Yeshua will restore where we fall short and remove our sin and desire to sin. We must never think we can handle our lives and relationships alone. Pride can creep up and damage our lives and relationships if we aren't careful to remain humble. We must uncover the layers beneath our surface. Instead, we can keep it covered, never to find the dead bones inside.

For instance, where there is one addiction, there is always another, if not three, four, or more. Those addictions pile up from dead bones beneath the surface. When it rains from hardships in someone's life, it can uncover some bones. But often, we throw more dirt on top of it to bury it deeper. One can turn to alcohol when life becomes stressful at work, with kids, or in marriage. When alcohol isn't helpful, they can distract themselves and become workaholics. They put all their effort, time, and energy into working and making money. When that's not enough, one may turn to drugs, porn, sex out of marriage, weed, cigarettes, or maybe even a combination. One addiction will always lead to another. While life becomes harder to navigate, like a broken GPS, one can become lost within themselves. We must uncover those dead bones and face the skeletons in the closet to discover who we are. We must learn to cope with a healthy heart, soul, body, and mind.

Deep down in our souls, the greatest desire is God, yet we replace the desire with some ingredient of the world to bring us pleasure. For us, the world is like baking a cake. We want to add more sugar to the batter to increase the sweetness. Likewise, we can seek to add more fleshly pleasure or sinful desires to our lives. Anyone I know would enjoy tasting good food rather than something nasty or burnt. So why not become the flavor that tastes good to God and your neighbor? Matthew 5:13 "You are the salt of the earth. But if the salt loses its saltiness, how can it be made salty again? It is no longer good for anything except to be thrown out and trampled underfoot."

Cake or cookies can taste gross if they do not have salt in their batter. Even the most minor amount of salt can bring out the most flavor. Don't let the world steal your salt or choose to become sugar. Sugar is easy to mix, but the salt takes longer to dissolve. The world is full of sugar, and everyone loves it. Likewise, the things in the world people love to enjoy, yet deep down, the body still craves salt. Without salt, we cannot survive, as our entire bodies will begin to fall apart until we eventually die. If we don't have salt to give others or to use within ourselves, we will lose the most essential ingredient in the world, and our insides will fall apart.

Leviticus 2:13 says, "Every offering of your grain offering you shall season with salt; you shall not allow the salt of the covenant of your God to be lacking from your grain offering." Even the offerings to God must be seasoned with salt. The grain offerings represent the comparison of the wheat from the tares. Our grain offerings should be our deeds to God. The servants of God begin to speak about the tares amongst the wheat. "Do you want us to go and pull them up?'" Matthew 13:29 "' No,' he answered, 'because while you are pulling the weeds, you may uproot the wheat with them." Here God is saying to let the wheat and tares grow together until the time of the harvest. This verse shows that God's workers are sown among the others in the world. No one can distinguish a wheat from a tare until the ripening of the fruit. How much more should we be careful so we don't accidentally pull the wicked up along with the righteous?

The Sea of Galilee and the Dead Sea are located in Israel. Between them is the Jordan River, which carries fresh water to the Dead Sea. The Galilee means a circle that bears freshwater and bursts forth with life. The Jordan means flowing down as we find new life and give out. We provide water to the dead sea, which means death in Hebrew, where nothing is living. These all give us an extensive picture like a road map. We first circle around the world to find new life, flow down and become baptized in the Spirit like Yeshua and John, then give out life to the dead.

Interestingly, we must become dead to receive salt, like the dead sea that flows with an abundance of salt. The salt in the Dead Sea is used worldwide for body washes, exfoliators, scrubs, body wraps, and polishers. It's used to benefit the body and help contribute to healthy living. The dead sea may give to the body but doesn't contribute to the soul.

The Sea of Galilee birthed Yeshua and brought the Spirit of God flowing through baptism in the Jordan to bring life to the dead sea. The spiritual salt can be used in offerings to God to season the grain offerings like wheat or baked cakes, as Leviticus 2 states in more detail. Without salt and grain offerings representing our fruitfulness, we can not be pleasing to God. The grain offerings represent our worship to God and our love for his ultimate sacrifice. Yeshua says, "Unless a kernel of wheat falls to the ground and dies, it remains only a single seed." We must be born again to die as a seed, to be brought to life and be baptized in His Holy Spirit. Continue to be fruitful and give life to the living like flowing water while keeping the flavor of salt and not sugar. Remember, God did not say to obtain sugar for the sacrifices but salt.

Psalm 107:33-34 "He changes rivers into a wilderness and springs of water into a thirsty ground; A fruitful land into a salt waste, Because of the wickedness of those who dwell in it." If we live in sin, the internal living waters from Galilee and the Jordan can become dried up and dead, only producing salt. Salt is good, but it comes with a greater offering. If the salt loses its flavor, the world tramples it underfoot and loses its value.

Layers of dirt and rock deeply cover the archeological findings in Israel. The geologists carefully remove layers to reveal the artifacts from the ground. In turn, we learn more about the historical culture and truths about the times of the Bible and ancient history. Likewise, we must have the hardened rock and dust within ourselves uncovered to reveal a deeper understanding of God's purpose for us according to his everlasting Spirit before creation.

Remember, it is said in Genesis 1:2, "the spirit hovered over the face of the waters"? We can skip ahead in the Bible and make a connection to the act of being physically baptized in water. We receive the Holy Spirit and shine the light God has given us since the beginning of creation. Yeshua teaches the concept of being the light on a hill after first serving as the salt of the world. It is important that we don't let go of our salt or stop shining our light in this world.

According to Ezekiel 47, when Yeshua returns, the Dead Sea will transform into a source of life and turn into fresh water. Recent discoveries in Israel's Dead Sea have revealed living fish populations, and there are signs that life may soon flourish throughout the previously barren region. Ezekiel 47:11 says, "Its swamps and marshes will not become fresh; they will be left for salt." The stagnant waters, those who practice their faith without action, will become salt and dry up. An inactive and unproductive soul will not be useful for the kingdom of God. Their lack of vitality in their soul creates stagnant waters that can foster mold, bacteria, and mosquitoes. However, God will transform others into fresh water and utilize them for a greater purpose. Verse 9 says, "There will be large numbers of fish because this water flows there and makes the salt water fresh; so where the river flows, everything will live." And verse 12 states, "Fruit trees of all kinds will grow on both banks of the river. Their leaves will not wither, nor will their fruit fail. Every month they will bear fruit because the water from the sanctuary flows to them. Their fruit will serve for food and their leaves for healing."

God says fruitful trees will grow along the river, which reminds me of David speaking about a tree planted beside still waters. As Psalm 92:13-16 says, "The righteous will flourish like a palm tree. He will grow like a cedar in Lebanon. Planted in the House of Adonai, they will flourish in the courts of our God. They will still yield fruit in old age. They will be full of sap and freshness. They declare, "Adonai is upright, my rock there is no injustice in Him." And 1 Peter 2:22 says, "He (Jesus) committed no sin, and no deceit was found in his mouth." The righteous who believe in Yeshua will bear fruit, flourishing and firmly planted like a tree in the temple of God. Revelation 14:5 says, "In their mouth was found no guile: for they are without fault before the throne of God." They will rest like a tree in His temple by believing in the name of Yeshua and feel confident approaching the throne. Hebrews 4:16 says, "Let us, therefore, come boldly unto the throne of grace, that we may obtain mercy, and find grace to help in time of need."

In times of need, know that God is always there to offer help and support, regardless of your current situation. Hebrews 5:1 "For every high priest taken from among men is appointed on behalf of people in things pertaining to God, in order to offer both gifts and sacrifices for sins." Our high priest, Yeshua, has offered a pleasing sacrifice to God, who can sympathize with us in our moments of weakness. Hebrews 5:8-9 says, "Although He was a Son, He learned obedience from the things which He suffered. And having been perfected, He became the source of eternal salvation for all those who obey Him." We should fasten the buckle of righteousness, direct our thoughts, and gaze toward the higher things.

Mark 9:49 says, "For everyone shall be salted with fire, and every sacrifice shall be salted with salt." And 1 Corinthians 3:13 states, "Every man's work shall be made manifest: for the day shall declare it, because it shall be revealed by fire; and the fire shall try every man's work of what sort it is." Then Colossians 4:6 says, "Let your speech always be with grace, as though seasoned with salt so that you will know how you should respond to each person." May we infuse all our actions with salt, the intention of love, and the fear and reverence of entering His temple on Yom Kippur (the Day of Repentance). May our lives be like a devoted priest serving in the temple, finding the greatest joy in offering praise and worship to Adonai, our God.

In the story of the good Samaritan, a man was beaten, robbed, and left to die. A priest journeyed along the road and passed him by. A Levite traveled on the road and passed him by. Finally, a Samaritan came by and compassionately stopped to bandage his wounds with wine and oil. The Samaritan was regarded as the proletariat and went out of his way to care for the man in need. He generously covered the cost of the man's stay at an inn, and not only that but provided additional financial support to alleviate the man's pain and discomfort. The Samaritan offered to reimburse extra if the man spent more than he supplied. The Levite and the priest could have lost income and work days from serving in the temple. According to Numbers 19:11-13, "Whoever touches a human corpse will be unclean for seven days. They must purify themselves with the water on the third day and on the seventh day; then they will be clean. But if they do not purify themselves on the third and seventh days, they will not be clean. If they fail to purify themselves after touching a human corpse, they defile the Lord's tabernacle. They must be cut off from Israel. Because the water of cleansing has not been sprinkled on them, they are unclean; their uncleanness remains on them."

The Levite and priest treated him as dead rather than offering care or assistance. They prioritized their pay and job duties over displaying kindness and affection. In contrast, the Samaritan did not have a role in the Jerusalem temple. Their background was a mix of Jewish and Gentile heritage, with their traditions and beliefs stemming from God's teachings. Despite the possibility of losing money, he acted out of compassion by offering all he had, including his donkey, wine, and oil, to show love and kindness. He wasn't living amidst stagnant waters. Instead, he was flourishing with vitality. It's not about religious works but having a sincere heart to serve God and love others. Allow the living waters to flow through you like fruit-bearing trees on all sides.

Love is more than just a feeling. It's a series of actions. Without action, can one honestly say that they are living in love? Love is demonstrated through acts of kindness, respect, giving, helping, showing compassion, reading God's word, obeying his commands, gentleness, humility, and caring for one another. These actions make love a verb and not just a passive emotion. A person possessing the fruits of the Spirit can produce living waters. As a result, their temple is filled with love and peace.

I recall a brother accompanying me on numerous mission trips. He consistently distributed tracts and engaged with people discreetly, almost like reading an iSpy book. He reminded me of the Good Samaritan who showed love, care, and gentleness to those others avoided and ignored. Most people tend to miss those individuals unless they are staring off into the vast unknown. Possessing compassion and love are the most valuable things a person can acquire in life. Without them, we may not understand the whole essence of God.

The individuals who have had the greatest impact on my life are not the wealthy, highly educated, famous, popular, or well-liked. Rather, they are those who could never reciprocate my kindness, and I could never repay them. As Luke 14:12-24 says, "When you give a banquet, invite the poor, the crippled, the lame, the blind, and you will be blessed. Although they cannot repay you, you will be repaid at the resurrection of the righteous." Truly those who can't repay in tangible matters, repayment is much greater in life by their hearts for God and others. The person who lives with compassion and loves the poor, the suffering, and the disabled God will bless in eternity.

The most awe-inspiring miracles I've ever seen didn't happen in crowded mega-churches or during speeches in stadiums about God - they occurred in the actions of individuals who went unnoticed. But God in heaven notices the soul with the characteristics written in Matthew 5. The meek, humble, merciful, pure in heart, peacemakers, mourners, poor in Spirit, that hunger and thirst for righteousness.

I'm reminded of a man who listened to me preach. He lived in a densely populated city in Europe. I was sharing a message for people to get alone in a quiet place with God, like a closet, a serene nature setting like an open field, a mountain, the ocean, or any other peaceful location. He felt as if God was speaking to him and decided to go to an open field to sit and wait on Him there. Earlier, I mentioned finding solitude, and it seems he found it. He had never experienced such peace, love, and joy. While praying to God, he discovered the treasure within the field he had been missing. Currently, there is a prevailing message to stockpile gold and other financial resources. However, it is vital to consider the value of storing the word of God in one's heart and exploring the priceless assets found in the Bible. These treasures are more valuable than any currency or material possession.

I reflect back on the story of Yeshua multiplying the fish and loaves in the open field. The people who gathered around him were hungry and thirsty, some seeking righteousness and others simply looking to satisfy their hunger. While Yeshua discerned their heart's intentions and said, "Amen, amen I tell you, you seek Me not because you saw signs, but because you ate all the bread and were filled. Don't work for food that spoils, but for the food that endures to eternal life, which the Son of Man will give to you. For on Him, God the Father has put the seal of approval." One who has the seal of God is not laboring and working for things that perish in this life but rather for eternal life. Those people thought they were seeking Jesus and God in heaven when they were blind to their intentions and seeking their stomach's desire.

I have observed similar situations in other countries as well as our own, where individuals only come together to receive offerings or donations. Some seek to obtain things such as food or money, but others are genuine in their desire for the bread of life. I saw a Jamaican woman whom God had directed me to approach and speak to. "What can I do for you?" Her eyes grew big as we began to talk. She said, "Give me a message. I know you are a man of God and a prophet sent from God." I stood quiet. Staring at this woman, I heard God speak to me. I told her, "I'm nobody but a man." She says, "Sir, don't lie to me. You're a prophet because God told me he sent you." I told her exactly what God told me to say. At first, she was a little combative, and then she broke into tears and began to thank me and God. I was moved with compassion and offered to give her any money, and she said, "Sir, please don't do that! I don't need money, nor does anyone else! What they need is the word of God, the bread of life!" She said it perfectly: people need the bread of life, not more money!

As it's written in John 6:35-36. "Yeshua said to them, "I am the bread of life. Whoever comes to Me will never be hungry, and whoever believes in Me will never be thirsty. But I told you that you have seen Me, yet you do not believe." Despite witnessing the signs and miracles of the multiplied loaves of bread and fish, they still refused to believe. God can provide you with money, food, and resources, but those living for their bellies and the world will often still not believe. The ones who will believe are those Yeshua says to gather for the banquet; the poor, the blind, the crippled, and the lame.

Luke 14:18-24 mentions gathering these humble and hurting people. But before asking these people, the servant first asked one man who said, "I just bought a farm." Another said, "I just bought five teams of oxen." While another said, "I just got married." All of these represent individuals' hearts in the world. One bought property, house, or farm. While another just started a job or started a business. The other was focused on a new marriage or relationship. All asked the servant to have them excused from joining God's banquet. How many can ignore time with God in their heart by giving God crumbs from their 5-course dinner plate because they spent time pursuing other goals? God sends his servants to those who are disabled, broken, hurting, blind, and suffering from mental and health issues. Isn't it fascinating that we are seeing this exact scenario today?

If Jesus walked into a modern-day church and sat in the back, hardly anyone would greet, recognize, or acknowledge him. Unfortunately, many people today are only interested in physical matters and miracles, like fish, bread, success, and marriage. They do not seek spiritual nourishment from the manna and bread of life given by the Spirit of God through his teachings. 2 Peter 3:9 "The Lord is not slow in keeping his promise, as some understand slowness. Instead, he is patient with you, not wanting anyone to perish, but everyone to come to repentance." As we continue in Matthew 19:29, "Everyone who has left houses or brothers or sisters or father or mother or children or lands, for my name's sake, will receive a hundredfold and will inherit eternal life." He's not saying to abandon your family or house and begin to live as someone homeless. He's saying not to let these things hold you back from seeking him and his kingdom. It's revealed in Luke 5:11 "When they had brought their boats ashore, they left everything and followed Him." Don't you see the sacrifice of one's desire to relinquish their affection for worldly possessions and instead turn towards the worship of the one true God? Think about this in Luke 9:57-58 "Now it happened as they journeyed on the road, that someone said to Him, "Lord, I will follow You wherever You go." And Yeshua told him, "Foxes have holes, and birds of the air have nests, but the Son of Man has nowhere to lay His head."

Abraham understood this as Hebrews 11:10 says, "For he was looking forward to the city with foundations, whose architect and builder is God." Some people only build their homes on the ground, thinking it's the only option and this is their permanent home. But they don't realize the endless possibilities that exist in the infinite space of eternity, where no human-made structure can compare. Eternity remains a mystery beyond human comprehension. Its foundations and structures elude our grasp. To find God and his treasure, one must follow in the footsteps of the man who left the city, seeking refuge from the chaos of daily life. He sought after a life where human hands cannot erect any buildings, nor can the word of God be fashioned by our own design. The word spoken by God is not something temporal but something eternal that can be discovered from within and above.

CHAPTER 10

From Death To Life

In the blink of an eye, my life had taken a turn for the worst. I faced a challenge that no one could explain, not even the most knowledgeable doctors or specialists. For over a year and a half, I had been plagued by an unknown illness that left me feeling weak, nauseous, and excruciating pain. It wasn't until I found myself lying in a hospital bed at Emory Hospital in Atlanta, Georgia, that I realized just how serious my condition was. As I lay there gasping for air, my heart racing and my body wracked with pain; I knew something was seriously wrong. An EKG revealed that my heart skipped beats and my liver was in severe pain. My oxygen levels were dangerously low, and I felt like the entire room was spinning out of control. My heart sank when the doctor entered the room and told me they didn't know what was wrong. I felt like I was about to die at any moment. But then, something miraculous happened. As I stared at my two small children and my wife, I had a sudden flash of a vision. I saw myself healthy and strong, surrounded by my loved ones, and I knew I had to fight for my life. I started praying to God, asking for strength and guidance, and feeling a sense of peace over me.

Despite the uncertainty and fear that I felt, I knew that I had to keep fighting. I refused to give up, even when the odds seemed stacked against me. And in the end, my determination and faith paid off. I overcame my illness and emerged stronger and more resilient than ever.

God gave me a vision at that exact moment, and I was shown a world of lost souls. The very leaders who were meant to guide the lost were leading them more astray, and I watched in horror as thousands of disheartened people were led to the slaughter. Their sadness and depression weighed heavily on my heart, and I knew I had to do something to help them. With tears in my eyes, I begged God for a chance to make a difference, even if it meant sacrificing everything I had. I prayed, "Whatever it takes, and no matter what I have to go through, no matter how much I have to suffer, I want to be used for your glory to save these people." As I prayed, I opened my phone, and two notifications appeared. Then the doctor returned with a possible diagnosis of Lyme Disease. It was a shock but also an answer to my prayers.

I remembered being bit by a tick long ago, and now I knew what was causing my suffering. But this was only the beginning of my journey. As I underwent tests and treatments for Lyme Disease and its many coinfections, I faced the greatest battle of my life. It was a struggle that tested my faith and my strength, but it was also a journey that brought me closer to God than ever before. And in the midst of my pain and suffering, I discovered something incredible. Despite my illness, God was using me to do His work. Through my struggles, I could reach out to others who were suffering and offer them hope and comfort. It was the most incredible work I had ever done, all because of this chronic illness that had once threatened to destroy me. As I look back on my journey, I am filled with gratitude for the trials that brought me to where

I am today. I know that God has a plan for me. I believe He will continue to use me to make a difference in the world. And I am ready to face whatever challenges come my way, knowing I can overcome anything with God.

Through my many trials, I have witnessed God's transformative power in countless individuals' lives. Addictions to porn, alcohol, and drugs have been broken. Marriages on the brink of collapse have been restored to health. Sex addicts have found freedom, and homosexuals have been released from same-sex desires. Even the most brutal gang members have been delivered from sin by the power of Jesus. I learned the power of God in my weakness! Like Paul, I have understood that His grace is sufficient for me and that His strength is perfect in my weakness. 2 Corinthians 12:9, "My grace is sufficient for you, for my power is made perfect in weakness. Therefore I will boast all the more gladly about my weaknesses so that Christ's power may rest on me."

Oh, have I ever understood the words of Paul even more so now? While persevering through other professing believers tearing me down like Job's friends and saying many hurtful words toward me with judgment. Paul did not let his illness affect his perseverance in the work for the Lord. Paul says in Galatians 4:13-14 "As you know, it was because of an illness that I first preached the gospel to you, and even though my illness was a trial to you, you did not treat me with contempt or scorn. Instead, you welcomed me as if I were an angel of God, as if I were Yeshua the Messiah himself." I am thinking back on a sermon I gave in front of people while this verse speaks like a vision in my frontal lobe.

I had shortness of breath and air hunger from Babesia, which took away my oxygen and infiltrated my red blood cells like malaria. Yet, amidst it all, God gave one of the most life-giving sermons likely to leave my flesh dying. Through visions of people struggling with internal battles from lying on that hospital bed, I have seen souls surrender their lives to Jesus. And so I praise God for His transformative power and the privilege of witnessing His work in the lives of those around me. Praise God!

As I ponder the word of Paul in Philippians 4:13, "I can do all things through Christ who strengthens me." The depth of his suffering strikes me. In the verse before, he says, "I know what it is to be in need, and I know what it is to have plenty. I have learned the secret of being content in any and every situation, whether well fed or hungry, whether living in plenty or in want." But this contentment did not come easily. Paul endured beatings, mockery, shipwrecks, starvation, imprisonment, illness, and stoning. Through it all, he discovered the strength of God and how to find contentment no matter what life threw his way.

Paul says in Philippians 4:8, "Whatever is true, whatever is noble, whatever is right, whatever is pure, whatever is lovely, whatever is admirable if anything is excellent or praiseworthy think about such things." He speaks from experience, knowing that even the most brutal hardships cannot outweigh the strength of God. The most extraordinary veterans aren't given a purple heart for sitting back and watching, but for those who sacrificed their life and paid the ultimate price in the line of duty. In the kingdom of God, the most outstanding award will go to those who face challenges and suffer for their faith and God's will. Those who play church, live for the world and avoid the spiritual battle that shapes us into God's image will only receive a virtual medal of honor. The purple heart is reserved for those who have put their lives on the line for God and others. Let us follow in the footsteps of Paul, who endured great suffering but found strength and contentment in Christ. May we be willing to sacrifice everything for the gospel's sake, knowing that the reward in Heaven will far outweigh any hardship we face on Earth.

What is honor worth in a virtual world for you and those in the virtual reality with you? You aren't receiving the recognition on Memorial Day or Veterans Day in real life because your medals are fake from a virtual world. Yet, some seem lost in this virtual reality, chasing after fleeting pleasures and false beliefs. They are trapped in a world of their own making, where pursuing earthly desires is the only goal. But for those who live for the Holy Spirit, this life is a mere shadow of the everlasting existence that awaits them. They are not bound by the constraints of this world, like a VR headset or a video game. Instead, they fight a spiritual battle, a war for eternity. Those trapped in the world's game are like children lost in a fairytale, watching Disney movies or playing Call of Duty. Their lives are no different than scrolling through social media, pretending to be holy, or chasing after wealth and fame. They are enslaved to their desires, with no true battles to fight except the constant struggle with their flesh.

The Bible says in Acts 19:15, "But the evil spirit answered them, "Jesus I know, and Paul I recognize, but who are you?" The seven sons of Sceva tried to mimic the Holy Spirit by invoking the name of Jesus and casting out demons. Isn't that interesting that they knew Yeshua and Paul but didn't know those Seven? How could this be? These seven played church. They were no different than those playing Call of Duty and spending their lives on social media. It's all fake, imaginary, no real war, a game—all a virtual reality. As a result, verse 16 says, "Then the man who had the evil Spirit jumped on them and overpowered them all. He gave them such a beating that they ran out of the house naked and bleeding." The seven sons were no threat to Satan's kingdom on Earth. But Paul and Yeshua shook all of hell and the entire Earth! They had an enormous impact on Earth, larger than the two atomic bombs that were dropped on Hiroshima and Nagasaki in Japan during World War II. Paul and Yeshua would have saved the 129,000 and 226,000 from death in those cities of Japan, like Jonah, who warned Nineveh to repent of their sin and idolatry, estimated to be 120,000 people.

Imagine the uproar that would ensue in the fiery depths of hell if a single soul or a multitude were to turn away from their wicked ways and repent. Similarly, to what extent do you believe that the devil and his demons know the soul that destroys the lives of numerous individuals through sin or worldly influences? The devil remains unperturbed and impervious to the actions of those who merely play at being religious, fail to teach accurately, pray infrequently, prioritize worldly pursuits, engage in sin, pursue wealth, and lead a spiritually unproductive life. Conversely, the devil recognizes and acknowledges those who pray earnestly, teach sound doctrine, proclaim God's word, live as light, and exhibit righteous behavior in accordance with the fruits of the Spirit. The demons within a particular individual recognized Yeshua and Paul but not the seven sons of Sceva. These demons overpowered the seven men, leaving them naked and wounded, symbolizing the spiritual state of those who live according to the flesh rather than the Spirit. Such individuals lack the necessary spiritual armor to combat the enemy and challenge his malevolent dominion. They cannot wage a genuine war while merely engaging in a virtual one. Those who suffer the most in this life, who serve God's kingdom most fervently, will be recognized and overcome the devil's empire in hell.

People who experience suffering have a profound understanding that transcends the roughly 6,500 languages spoken on Earth. Understanding the language of pain is rarer than Rhodium, Iridium, and Ruthenium, some of Earth's most scarce commodities. Enduring suffering is considered valuable in God's kingdom, and it is uncommon for anyone not to experience it before entering eternity. One example that comes to mind is Elisha, a prophet who possessed twice the amount of the Holy Spirit that Elijah had. Both performed remarkable signs, miracles, and wonders through the power of God. However, Elisha passed away due to an illness at the end of his life. Was his death a result of wrongdoing, sin, or lack of faith? Certainly not!

Elisha completed the mission on Earth as God says in Isaiah 57:1 "The righteous perishes, and no man takes it to heart; Merciful men are taken away, while no one considers that the righteous is taken away from evil." God, who is just and merciful, has taken away evil from the world in the past, just as he did with Elijah and Enoch. Living for the flesh in the Earth's virtual reality, the worldly can not comprehend why God allows the righteous and merciful to become sick or face death. They often assume it's because of sin or lack of faith. In Matthew 7:1-6 Yeshua says, "Do not judge; in the same way you judge others, you will be judged." That isn't very comforting. Matthew 5:7 says, "Blessed are the merciful, for they shall obtain mercy." God says that if we judge, we might miss the log in our eye while seeing the speck in our neighbor's eye. God will judge us in the same manner as we judge others. However, if we display mercy, God will also show mercy to us when we stand before his throne.

Proverbs 28:3 says, "Whoever conceals his transgressions will not prosper, but he who confesses and forsakes them will obtain mercy." We can view this verse from the same perspective as judging. We can often conceal sins deep within and judge our neighbors through the same sins. Instead, shouldn't we be like the tax collector in Luke 18:13? "Who stood at a distance, he would not even look up to Heaven, but beat his breast and said, 'God, have mercy on me, a sinner." Shouldn't we show compassion and mercy when approaching someone before passing judgment on their precious soul?

I contemplate the many trials and tribulations God has placed before me. When I was young, two of my grandmothers passed away in the same year. As I grew older, I had 30% hearing in one ear and 70% in the other. Now God has restored the hearing in both of my ears to 100%. I once had seizures, and an MRI showed a dark spot in my brain. Now God has healed me from seizures. The greatest language I could ever learn is suffering and suffering with those suffering. I learned not to judge but to see through the eyes of mercy. It's like someone with terrible eyesight decides to undergo Lasik surgery. When people are tired of wearing manufactured glasses and contacts, they have Lasik surgery.

Can you imagine if every believer judged someone wearing glasses and contacts, claiming it's because of sin or lack of faith? Is that the love and mercy of Yeshua and his Spirit? Of course not! Yeshua went to heal people who were blind while no one else would heal them. Those judging someone's condition have not been made whole in the love of God. Remember the layers I mentioned in the previous chapters that someone must uncover? God must remove the layers before we receive His healing. Our role is to foster encouragement and love rather than passing judgment. Someone full of God's love will pray for others and be there for the one suffering. It's easy to rejoice with those rejoicing, but how many can suffer along with those suffering? Romans 12:5 "Rejoice with them that do rejoice, and weep with them that weep."

In Luke 19:41-44, Yeshua lamented the impending destruction of Jerusalem and the consequent suffering that would befall its inhabitants due to their rejection of his message of peace and salvation. Yeshua also wept in John 11:21. "Lord," Martha said to Yeshua, "If you had been here, my brother would not have died." When Lazarus passed away, Yeshua noticed Mary, Martha, and the others with them mourning, crying, and grieving. He, too, felt their pain and shed tears for their sorrow. Although he knew he would raise Lazarus from the dead to show his power for the kingdom to come, he was deeply moved by the pain of others' sorrow and suffering. Even in death, Lazarus was not deaf to the voice of God. His Spirit, though separated from his body, was attuned to the voice of the Almighty, resonating with a faith that surpassed all the living. For in that moment of transcendence, Lazarus was not merely a corpse, but a vessel of unwavering faith, a testament to the power of God to overcome death.

We know that Yeshua cried for people's lack of faith, his coming suffering, and the pain of others. We all should also have the same heart, and God's Lasik surgery called Mercy Eyes to eliminate Earth's manufactured human-designed glasses and contact lenses. Philippians 2:4-5 says, "Let each of you look out not only for his own interests but also for the interests of others. Let this mind be in you, which was also in Yeshua the Messiah." Psalm 34:19 "Many are the afflictions of the righteous, but the Lord delivers him out of them all." Whether life or death, it's clear that the righteous will have many afflictions and sufferings. Paul understood this in Philippians 3:10, "That I may know him and the power of his resurrection, and may share his sufferings, becoming like him in his death."

Suffering brings death to the flesh, so we don't become too comfortable in Earth's shoes. Eventually, you must change your shoes when the soles get worn out. All living things have a 100% chance of dying, some sooner and some later. We can change the tires on a car when the tread becomes worn down, but eventually, the engine or transmission will break down. Throughout history, humankind has crafted countless inventions, from the humble shoe to the mighty automobile. Yet, despite their usefulness and ingenuity, all of these creations will eventually meet their end in a desolate junkyard or landfill. However, there is hope for some, as they may be salvaged and repurposed to create entirely new materials, breathing new life into what was once considered waste.

Our bodies are the same. We all will end up in a graveyard, but after the body dies, the soul will be wasted in hell or recycled in Heaven. Have you ever heard the phrase, "One man's trash is another man's treasure?" I think about the man on Joyxee Island off the coast of Cancun City, Mexico. This man ingeniously utilized discarded recyclables and waste to construct a miniature. While numerous individuals aspire to possess an island on Earth, this individual transformed what others deemed useless into a cherished dream. God's kingdom is the same. Certain individuals may overlook certain aspects of His word, dismissing them as insignificant. However, these overlooked elements may hold immense value to others, serving as a source of tranquility and personal fulfillment akin to a private dream island.

Remember the island that I spoke of earlier to envision in your mind? Build it with the bricks and stones of God's word and the discarded riches for God's kingdom thrown away by others to build up your foundation. As Matthew 13:12 says, "Whoever has will be given more, and they will have an abundance. Whoever does not have, even what they have will be taken from them." No sane soul would dare to discard precious metals or currency, yet why do we carelessly cast aside God's word? The most valuable treasure known to man lies within its pages, yet we treat it as mere refuse. It could be because we've yet to uncover the true riches hidden within its depths. Instead, we choose to place our faith in the fleeting treasures of this world.

Reflecting on my grandfather's legacy, I am reminded of the power and value of resources. He was a man of great intellect and ambition, with two master's degrees and a successful career as a Civil Engineer. But it was his ownership of coal mines that truly set him apart. His company was responsible for extracting the precious resources that fueled the world's energy and electricity needs. It was a profitable venture, and everyone clamored for a piece of the pie. My great uncle was a master inventor who crafted and patented countless innovations. His creations ranged from a device still utilized in the coal mining and oil and gas industries to a technology that enabled rocketships to soar through space. Yet, he also unwittingly devised a crucial component of the atomic bomb, a tool that would ultimately contribute to untold devastation. He understood the power of the resources and tools at his disposal, capable of uplifting and destroying society equally.

But as I ponder the significance of these resources, I am struck by the analogy to God's word. Just as coal was a valuable commodity, so is the Spirit of God, the most precious resource one can ever obtain. It is the key to eternal life and the foundation of our faith. Yeshua reminds us in Matthew 7:13-14 "Enter through the narrow gate. For wide is the gate and broad is the road that leads to destruction, and many enter through it. But small is the gate and narrow the road that leads to life, and only a few find it." It requires a willingness to labor and sacrifice, to enter through the narrow gate and follow the narrow road. Just as few were willing to brave the dangers of the coal mines or the sanctity of the temple, so too are few ready to pursue the Spirit of God with the same zeal and dedication.

For many, the allure of this life's luxuries is too great to resist. They want the benefits of coal or the temple's riches but are unwilling to do the hard work themselves. They seek shortcuts and easy paths, not realizing that value and meaning can only be found through perseverance and dedication. So let us not be like those who seek to steal or exploit the treasures of this world. Let us instead be like my grandfather, who understood the value of hard work and dedication. Let us enter through the narrow gate and follow the narrow road, knowing that the Spirit of God is the most valuable resource we can ever obtain. Only a select few possess the knowledge to transfigure the word of God into real-life circumstances or to wield the tools of the temple with the Spirit that lies within their very soul. The true purpose and potential of the Holy Spirit remain a mystery to most, as does the art of utilizing the word of God to its fullest extent in this human life.

Some know how to use the word of God and its tools and resources contained within, but they may also use the word for their devastation and destruction to themselves and others. We must treat the word of God with the utmost care as if it were a box marked "fragile" containing our most precious possessions. One wrong move, one careless shake, and the contents within will shatter into a million pieces, rendering them useless for their intended purpose. The words of God are like precious gems that have the power to transform our very souls. We must handle them with the utmost caution as if we were carrying bottles of nitroglycerin that could detonate at any moment.

The soul of a human is the most precious item, one that must be handled with the most care, whether it's your own or someone else's. We must tread lightly, for the power of our words can either build or destroy. It is imperative that we don't use God's word as a weapon to hurt or abuse others. Instead, we must nurture our souls, guarding them against the world's corrupting influences.

I am reminded of my two great-uncles, who were drafted to play for Major League Baseball. One chose to leave the Boston Red Sox to serve his country in the military, recognizing that protecting the freedoms of his fellow citizens and serving God was a greater calling than fame and fortune. The other obeyed his father and left the New York Yankees to become a teacher, imparting invaluable life lessons and teaching God's ways to the next generation. Their choices were not easy, but they were guided by a deep sense of purpose and a desire to impact the world positively. They understood that the soul is our most precious possession and must be nurtured and protected at all costs. May we all follow in their footsteps, using our words and actions to build up rather than tear down and guard our souls against the forces that seek to corrupt them.

The times in society have indeed drifted away from what matters most in life. Instead, people turn to prosperity, money, fame, success, and otherworldly vanity. They have traded the word of God and its values for the worship of mammon - the god of wealth and material possessions. Instead of prioritizing the well-being of their neighbor, they have succumbed to the allure of self-indulgence and self-love. The sacred bond of community has been shattered, replaced by a culture of greed and selfishness. It is a sorrowful state of affairs, as the true essence of humanity is lost amidst the pursuit of worldly pleasures.

The world appears to wear a VR headset while living in virtual reality, which has no purpose and meaning, nor does their life on Earth have value in contributing to eternity. We must break the VR headset and the false reality such as the news and social media, which no longer have a physical connection but a virtual Morse code by sharing videos and pictures devoted to oneself and selfish ambitions and desires, fueling the Tower of Babylon they have built inside their soul. One must ask themselves, "What is my purpose-driven life?" Deep down, what keeps your engines running and your feet walking ahead? What drives you to continue in life?

In early America, before big corporations took over, Jews would start businesses to help people and contribute to the well-being of others and society. Sadly, the motor of Babylon has driven humanity to build a bigger tower while others develop their tower alongside the tallest buildings. If one's motivation is not operated for a purpose by God, helping and loving your neighbor, one should have their engine evaluated with a diagnostic test. God is the mechanic in diagnosing engine problems that will later cause a breakdown in one's heart, soul, and mind. The brain can be compared to an engine, while the heart can be likened to a transmission. The Holy Spirit is the vital fluid that keeps the car running smoothly. As for the fuel, it can be represented by the word of God. We must drive around while operating in the Holy Spirit and allowing God's word to fill us to keep the engine and transmission running. Without the gas and fluids, the engine and transmission will not start. It will simply become an idle car sitting in the driveway. When someone has an issue with their vehicle, they take it to the mechanic to figure out the problem.

In the same way, we bring our hearts, soul, and mind to God: the mechanic and the greatest engineer in the universe, to troubleshoot the problem and fix the issue within. Lamentation 2:5 "Restore us to yourself, O Lord, that we may be restored! Renew our days as of old." Everyone will become downcast if their car has issues, especially if it breaks down. Many would love to have their car brand new again that's right off the factory line after it's been driven thousands of miles and reached many years of age. But only God has the power to restore all things. 2 Corinthians 5:17 "Therefore, if anyone is in Yeshua, he is a new creation. The old has passed away; behold, the new has come." The old car has become restored as the body has been renewed within us by His Holy Spirit. 2 Corinthians 7:1 says, "Since we have these promises, beloved, let us cleanse ourselves from every defilement of body and spirit, bringing holiness to completion in the fear of God." No human would buy or receive a new car and then purposely wreck it. So why ruin your body with sin that causes damage from within? You might as well put vegetable oil inside your engine to replace engine oil. Your engine will smoke until everything connected to the car becomes destroyed.

Some yearn for the latest cellphone, car, camera, tablet, toy, ATV, or laptop with an unquenchable thirst. However, once they finally obtain it, the initial thrill and euphoria only lasts for a fleeting moment, a mere few days to weeks, before it begins to depreciate. As the years go by, why not renew your heart, soul, and mind by upgrading to a new phone, car, camera, laptop, etc? God's word is like the upgrade to ensure we continue operating efficiently within our hearts and mind. Most people would prefer not to receive negative news about their heart, brain, or health conditions such as Alzheimer's or other serious illnesses from a doctor. Hearing those words can be unsettling, and they may ask their doctor, "What steps can I take to resolve this issue?" It's important to prioritize the health of your heart and mind by nourishing them with the power of the Holy Spirit. This way will ensure that your soul operates like a well-functioning device and that you renew yourself daily, just like an upgrade, to function more efficiently. Throughout life, we will suffer, but God has a plan for you if you continue firmly in the faith. 1 Peter 5:10 "The God of all grace, who called you to his eternal glory in Yeshua, after you have suffered a little while, will himself restore you and make you strong, firm and steadfast."

Life is a journey that leads us down unknown roads. Despite this uncertainty, there is one constant that never changes - God, who guides us like a compass. As we journey through life, we may alter our path from north to south, east to west, but the cardinal directions and the passage of time remain the same. While time moves forward, we can alter the path of our lives by investing our time in God or the world. However, the past is unchangeable, and we can only move forward by embracing the plan that God has in store for us.

Paul writes in Philippians 3:13-14 "Brothers, I do not consider that I have made it my own. But one thing I do: forgetting what lies behind and straining forward to what lies ahead, I press on toward the goal for the prize of the upward call of God in Yeshua the Messiah." Let us also do the same as we strive to finish the work God set before us to complete, like Moses and Yeshua, until the very end.

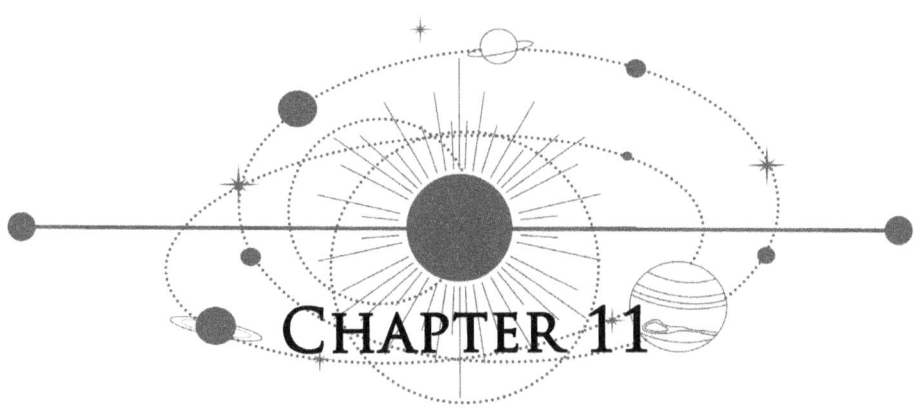

CHAPTER 11

Don't Leave My Presence

As I stood in Beit El, the ancient city of Bethel, a sudden cloud descended upon me and the two others with me. The Holy Spirit tugged at my heart, urging me to seek solitude. I ventured into the thick mist, walking until I found a spot to sit and pray. Time seemed to slip away as I communed with God, but as I rose to leave, I heard His voice loudly say, "Son, do not leave my presence." I turned to face the heavens, wondering at the source of the voice. I returned to where I was sitting, and then, I heard it again, a mournful weeping that shook me to my core, "Son, be careful not to leave my presence." The tears flowed freely from my eyes as I felt the overwhelming love of God surround me.

At that moment, I understood the depth of God's desire to be close to us, his most precious creation. He wept for the death that would come into the world and the pain and suffering we would endure. And yet, he knew that he must send his son to save us, to bring us back into his presence for all eternity. To, again, draw us near to His habitation where nothing unclean can stand. May we be restored to a relationship with God that is pure and true, and may we never forget the depth of his love for us. Matthew 5:8 "Blessed are the pure in heart, for they shall see God." We will see the face of God and who he is every day if we draw near to him with a pure heart.

Moses understood the presence of God. In Exodus 33:15,17, "Moses said to him [God], "If your Presence does not go with us, do not send us up from here." Then Adonai said to Moses, "I will also do this thing that you have spoken; for you have found grace in My sight, and I know you by name." Moses was pure in heart, and he was pleasing to God. Like Moses, Isaiah was also pure in heart, but he felt unclean, yet he was full of humility. Isaiah 6:5, "Woe is me! For I am lost; for I am a man of unclean lips, and I dwell in the midst of a people of unclean lips; for my eyes have seen the King, the Lord of hosts!" Isaiah and Moses were both humble and pure in heart.

Psalm 53:2 "God looks down from heaven on all mankind to see if there are any who understand, any who seek God." We see this in Moses' life when he saw the heart of Isaiah and said to him in verse 8, "Whom shall I send? And who will go for us?" And I said, "Here am I. Send me!" God is constantly looking for a vessel with a willing, humble, contrite, obedient, and pure heart to serve him in his temple. As a believer, you are considered God's temple and precious possession. He wants to keep you holy and pure, without any impurities so that you can be used for His divine purposes. In 1 Peter 2:9, Look here, "You are a chosen people, a royal priesthood, a holy nation, God's special possession, that you may declare the praises of him who called you out of darkness into his wonderful light." Isn't that beautiful? Many desire to see God, but who has seen him? 1 John 4:12 "No one has ever seen God; if we love one another, God abides in us, and his love is perfected in us." The only ones who will see God are those who love one another and allow his love to become perfected in them. God says, "If you love me, keep my commandments." God says that his commandments are not burdensome.

For example, idols were always heavy to carry. The only way to relocate them was to break them. Josiah understood this well in 2 Chronicles 34:33 as he destroyed all of Israel's idols, including Bethel and Dan, and the houses and temples where idol worship occurred. Why did he decide to smash and tear down the idols instead of choosing a different disposal method? God reveals the answer with Moses in Exodus 32:20 "He took the calf the people had made and burned it in the fire; then he ground it to powder, scattered it on the water and made the Israelites drink it." He neither held onto the gold nor tried to remake it into some other use for the flesh. He certainly wouldn't use it for service in God's temple or anyone else's financial benefit. He destroyed the idol just like Josiah did, ensuring it would never be used for any other purpose. The idols were destroyed and demolished in all locations where false worship occurred.

God is saying that you must destroy your idols and burdens in your life. You cannot carry sin, remake the idol of sin, or redesign sin into something good. Never resort to evil means for financial gain or to acquire something you would become excessively attached to. In America, people have houses but sometimes rent storage units to store more items. It's a massively profitable industry in America, but the problem is excessive materialism weighs one down. Like a full truck driving down the interstate, the speed at which one can travel is limited. Adding a trailer containing additional cargo further reduces the rate of travel. The destination you are heading to will take much longer than it would if you only drove a small moving truck. The same goes for a hiker with a heavy backpack. It will be much more challenging, exhausting, and slow down than if you had a light pack.

Likewise, the destination in life that God desires you to arrive at will take much longer than anticipated with the excessive heaviness of sin and idols in your life. As Hebrews 12:1 says, "Since we are surrounded by so great a cloud of witnesses, let us lay aside every weight, and the sin which so easily ensnares *us,* and let us run with endurance the race that is set before us." We must shed the burden of sin that holds us back and run with faith, emulating those in the Bible who conquered the world through faith, as Hebrews 11 reminds us. The cloud of witnesses is those who have overcome the world and sin by faith. It is those who have endured until the end and have died and risen to the heavens with God. The cloud that enveloped us at Bethel is a great representation.

Bethel was where Jacob received a dream from God, where angels ascended and descended from the heavens as John saw with Yeshua at the Jordan River, referenced in John 1:50-51. But Bethel was burned and destroyed. Once again, the power of God's word has triumphed over evil. The cloud of witnesses, who lived with obedience, trust, and faith, endured and overcame idolatry, false worship, and sin. Like Yeshua at the Transfiguration Mountain, he and his disciples became enveloped in a cloud with two witnesses, Elijah and Moses. The disciples witnessed Yeshua shining in the glory of God, foreshadowing what was to come for Him and all of us. He still had to conquer and overcome the world and everything in it to offer salvation to those who live by faith. 1 John 5:4 "For every child of God defeats this evil world, and we achieve this victory through our faith."

Let's dive deeper. James 2:26 says, "As the body without the spirit is dead, so faith without deeds is dead." Without the holy spirit, the body will not have eternal life in heaven. Without faith, one cannot live with good works according to heaven. Anyone can demonstrate kindness, generosity, and care for others, but how many possess these traits while loving God and avoiding sinful behavior, prioritizing money and worldly desires? Faith is a valuable commodity, and faith comes from hearing the word of God, not just by hearing but by doing what it says. James 1:23-24 says, "Anyone who listens to the word but does not do what it says is like someone who looks at his face in a mirror. You see yourself, walk away, and forget what you look like."

Have you ever thought about why you go through the same routine every morning, doing your hair or makeup, washing and cleaning your face, and brushing your teeth while looking at yourself in the mirror, only to forget what you look like? What would happen if you stopped taking care of yourself and neglected the actions I mentioned, including abandoning your morning routine? Have you ever wondered what would happen if you consistently worked out and monitored your progress by looking at yourself in the mirror and taking pictures but then stopped exercising for years? What if you had a job and suddenly stopped working, leading to losing everything while sitting at home? Wouldn't you stop doing any work for yourself and forget your former condition and what you have learned in the past? Where did you acquire the knowledge and skills to care for yourself, engage in physical activity, and be productive? Just like learning to care for your heart, soul, body, and mind, hearing and understanding the word of God is crucial. However, you can only exercise faith and care for your eternal soul when you put it into action. If a person listens to God's teachings but does not follow them, they are similar to someone who hires a personal trainer and a dietitian, exercises at the gym and tries to build muscle while frequently fasting for days and weeks. It's similar to a gym-goer trying to lose weight but continues to eat foods high in carbs, fast food, sugary treats, soda, and junk food. They may listen to advice about healthy eating but don't implement it.

Hebrew is the oldest language in civilization, contrary to scholars' and historians' theories and inaccurate carbon dating. Hebrew was the world's first language but is not the most valuable and essential language in God's kingdom. Before the fall of man, the Holy Spirit's language was already present. This speech comprises God's glory, praise, worship, and peace. It's the language of eternity and obedience to God without sin. It's being faithful to him and resisting the bite of worldly temptations.

The same tree that Adam and Eve ate the forbidden fruit from in the Garden of Eden is like the tree Judas betrayed Jesus and subsequently took his own life by hanging himself. The Tree of Knowledge of Good and Evil represents the desire to understand what was evil and understand the way God does. It's an unsatiable desire and craving for what is forbidden, which goes against God and his natural law and design in the universe.

Judas, once a loyal disciple, succumbed to the lure of greed and the tantalizing promise of a bribe. This insidious temptation led him down a path of darkness, causing him to inflict harm upon those around him. As his sins piled up, he was consumed by gnawing guilt yet unable to turn away from his wicked ways. Ultimately, the weight of his transgressions proved too much to bear, and he was left with nothing but the haunting temptation to end it all by hanging from a tree without ever seeking redemption. Thus he was cut off from the presence of God with no rest and peace. It's like sin brought in a category-five hurricane, destroying everything that was truly good and pleasant to one's soul.

I am reminded of the Israelites who were exiled to Babylon by God as a consequence of their sins, which also led to the destruction of Jerusalem. While in Babylon, the citizens asked the Israelites to "play a song of Zion." Psalm 137:4 they said, "How can we sing the Lord's song In a foreign land?" How can someone sincerely sing a song to Adonai while still in sin? It's unlikely that Adam and Eve sang hymns to God when they were banished from the Garden of Eden. However, many people did sing praises to Yeshua while he rode on a donkey into Jerusalem. The Israelites sang songs when God delivered the people from Egypt. It is said in the book of Revelation that people will sing even greater songs when he returns. Without having faith and trust in Yeshua, confessing his name, repenting from sins, and being born again, there is no hope or reason to celebrate in this world of Babylon. It's similar to the situation of the Israelites exiled in Babylon. They were so distressed and burdened by losing everything due to sin that they had no song to sing. What's the opposite of distress? Rest. What's the opposite of burden? Unburdened.

When someone repents and starts believing and living for Yeshua, the most common phrase I hear is, "I feel like a weight has been lifted from me." As Isaiah 10:27 says, "In that day their burden will be lifted from your shoulders, their yoke from your neck the yoke will be broken." God will lift the weight of the world's burdens and the heaviness of sin. God will relieve foreign nations from the burden of godlessness and break its influence over your life. The enemy will no longer be able to use you to construct or reconstruct its ruins. Joshua 6:26, we read that Joshua said, "Cursed before the Lord is the one who undertakes to rebuild this city, Jericho: "At the cost of his firstborn son he will lay its foundations; at the cost of his youngest he will set up its gates." We know that Hiel the Bethelite [from Bethel] rebuilt Jericho and lost his firstborn son. The general populace may perceive the verse mentioned as being severe. However, it must be noted that Jericho and its inhabitants were Canaanites who engaged in abhorrent practices such as pedophilia, bestiality, pederasty, prostitution, brutality, pornography, subjugation, inequity, homosexuality and transgenderism, idol worship, and abortion. Those who sought to reconstruct the ruins harbored similar motives. They were trying to rebuild the walls that created spiritual, physical, moral, mental, and emotional ruins in people's lives. The impact of witnessing the reconstruction of Jericho in various nations across the globe will undoubtedly elicit similar effects in the lives of individuals within society today.

Remember Rahab, a prostitute I spoke of in earlier chapters? She was from Jericho. Rahab placed her trust in God and turned away from her past actions, resulting in her life being spared. Furthermore, Yeshua was a descendant of Rahab, who God had purified. God didn't judge her or see her uncleanness, nor should anyone else. God transformed her into a beautiful soul. He helped remove her burdens, tore down the walls of Jericho in her life, and rebuilt the walls of the kingdom of heaven! Rahab was always beautiful, but now she can truly shine! God can do the same in your life regardless of what you did or who you were in the past. He desires no one to perish but to repent and come to His love.

God commanded the Israelites to avoid taking spoils and any possessions from Jericho. However, Achan rebelled against God's instructions and took the spoils for himself. Do you recall how Moses burned down the golden calf into powder and destroyed it earlier? God told everyone after destroying Jericho not to take the spoils. Achan didn't listen. He represents trying to hold onto the indulgence of sin, the lust of the eyes, pride, and greed for material possessions. Achan faced death to demonstrate the consequences if we took the spoils of sin for ourselves and denied our wrongdoing. The jewels are moldy and rotten fruit sitting in a bag with other healthy fruit. One moldy fruit will spread rapidly onto the others, ruining the entire batch. Likewise, a little leaven can ruin a whole batch of dough, and one sinner can begin to spoil many righteous and healthy souls. 1 Corinthians 15:33-34 "Do not be deceived: "Evil company corrupts good habits." Awake to righteousness, and do not sin; for some do not have the knowledge of God. I speak this to your shame."

The story of Korah's rebellion is one of greed, envy, and a thirst for power. In Numbers 16, 250 individuals conspired against Moses, driven by a desire to be praised by God more than their leader. But their aspirations were short-lived, as the ground beneath them opened up and swallowed them whole in what can only be described as a colossal sinkhole. A similar situation of deceit and betrayal occurred in the narrative of Ananias and Sapphira in Acts 5. After selling their land and promising to donate the proceeds to God, they kept a portion for themselves and only gave a fraction to the disciples. Their lies proved fatal, as they, too, met their demise. These examples serve as a warning that earthly desires can lead to destruction, both in body and soul. Only with the presence of God can one hope to avoid such a fate. They are sick and dying individuals that can destroy many people, like the walls of Jericho that reject healthy living with God and building up his kingdom.

If you are in good health and enter a doctor's office where many sick individuals are present, you will not catch their well-being but their illness. In the same way, one cannot attain a closer relationship with God in the midst of sin and ungodly behavior, like those who are unwell and do not prioritize their faith. Those who hunger for worldly experiences may have a higher likelihood of withstanding exposure to harmful substances such as mercury, arsenic, and lead than those who crave indulgent foods.

Sin is poisonous. If someone becomes poisoned or overdoses, they should call poison control. Likewise, one who overdoses on sin or drinks the world's influence of poison should call on heaven's poison control. Sin can cause a spiritual allergic reaction worse than someone allergic to bee stings. Without epinephrine, their throat may close, and they could enter anaphylactic shock. When sin takes hold of you and makes breathing difficult, the Holy Spirit of God acts like epinephrine to open your airways and clear your breathing. By obeying the teachings of God, you can protect yourself from spiritual harm caused by sinful behavior. It serves as a warning system, similar to the buzzing of bees, to alert you when temptation is near.

Take the vast open seas within the ocean with its roaring and crashing waves. One living in sin is like a small boat or raft that's drifted out into the ocean, becoming lost at sea. Feeling lost and uncertain about your direction can be a scary and isolating experience. It's natural to long for someone to come to your aid and guide you toward safety. Eventually, you become hungry, thirsty, weak, and tired while stuck out at sea. In the event of a storm, one's raft or boat may capsize due to large waves, necessitating a struggle for survival to avoid drowning. Sin is like a turbulent sea, relentlessly pounding against the shores of your heart, soul, and mind, leaving you gasping for air and struggling to stay afloat. And just when you think you've caught your breath, ravenous sharks lurking beneath the surface, biding their time with razor-sharp teeth, ready to pounce and consume you whole. As you fall into the ocean of sin and lose grip of the last comfort and security that kept you afloat, the devil and his demons are the sharks waiting to feast upon your drowning sinful flesh.

How much should one desire to rest on dry ground, without storms, on a tropical island with peace all around them during these moments? This visual of a solid foundation is the peace that God offers, and he will rescue you from the rough seas. Romans 10:13 "Everyone who calls on the name of the Lord will be saved." Avoid drifting out in the sea of sin and drowning in the storms, cast away from God's presence. 1 Corinthians 10:13 "No temptation has seized you beyond what people normally experience, and God can be trusted not to allow you to be tempted beyond what you can bear. On the contrary, along with the temptation he will also provide the way out, so that you will be able to endure." One can be saved and rescued by calling upon the name of Jesus. Keeping the word of God in the heart and mind, and trusting in it with guidance from the Holy Spirit, can help overcome temptation, just as Yeshua did in the desert when the devil twisted the word of God from Deuteronomy out of context.

The devil does not harbor trepidation towards individuals who simply commit scripture to memory. Rather, he is apprehensive of those who embody faith and ingrain the words within their heart, soul, and mind, firmly rooted in a solid foundation. God says in Micah 7:9, "Once again you will have compassion on us. You will trample our sins under your feet and throw them into the depths of the ocean!" If God has taken away your guilt, shame, and the weight of sin by casting it to the depths of the sea, do not attempt to dive down to retrieve it. Seek refuge in God, just as the U.S. Coast Guard rescues people from the jaws of sharks and brings them to a place of safety and security. Therein lies the calmness and steadfastness that comes with obedience and faith.

In the book of Genesis, chapter three, verse nine, we find God seeking out Adam with a poignant question: "Where are you?" Though the Almighty knew Adam's physical whereabouts, their once unbreakable bond had been shattered, leaving God with deep sorrow. He repeated the question, "Where are you?" to ask why Adam was no longer in his rightful place by God's side. The devil first whispered doubt into Adam and Eve's ears, asking, "Did God really say?" This insidious tactic is still used today, as the enemy seeks to lure us away from the presence of God. We must be vigilant and never question what God has already spoken. If we do, we risk losing the most precious relationship of all.

Imagine you're working in a bustling manufacturing or distribution facility, and one of the machines has gone haywire. A Lock Out Tag Out has been put in place to safeguard whoever is tasked with fixing the machine. But what if, in a moment of recklessness, you decide to remove the tag, break the lock, and flip the switch on? The consequences could be catastrophic - not only for the person working on the machine but for you as well. Similarly, God has set forth rules and laws to protect us from harm. Just as the Lock Out Tag Out is a safety measure, God's guidance is meant to keep us from injuring our souls. If we choose to ignore these safeguards and question the wisdom of God's plan, we risk causing irreparable damage to ourselves and those around us. So let us heed the warnings and trust in the protection set before us for our benefit.

In the text of Deuteronomy 17:19, it is written that a king must not only uphold the laws but also inscribe them and recite them daily. This practice is meant to instill a deep reverence for God and his commandments, which would prevent oppression, wickedness, injustice, disobedience, or immorality through the land and the lives of others. The reward for such devotion would be a state of peace and security for all. Every political system today has strayed from God's ways. Instead of seeking to honor God and serve the people, many leaders are driven by their selfish ambitions. They are like the builders of Babylon's tower, consumed by the pursuit of personal gain and worldly success.

2 Timothy 3:1-5 describes the characteristics of many in the last days and how they are reflected in today's society. We witness Isaiah 5:20 come to life and reflect on 2 Timothy 3, and our world turns upside down. "Woe to those who call evil good and good evil, who put darkness for light and light for darkness, who put bitter for sweet and sweet for bitter!" God's ways are for our protection and peace so that we know how to live and treat each other and ourselves. Throughout all of history, God has provided us with laws that encompass proper sanitation and hygiene, as well as guidelines on growing crops, cooking and consuming food, and appropriately disposing of waste, including excrement from bathroom use. God commands us only to eat meat cooked over the fire to ensure that all germs and bacteria are adequately killed. Otherwise, there is a risk of falling ill. He provided us with guidance on the appropriate timing for planting and harvesting crops to ensure that the seeds do not perish and the yields are not picked too late, which could lead to the growth of mold and other harmful bacteria. God has instructed us on how to properly sanitize and maintain good hygiene for the safety of ourselves and others. During the pandemic, many individuals were advised by doctors and the media to adopt more rigorous hygiene and disinfection practices. How much more should we keep these things in practice when God has been telling us to since the beginning?

Why did people in ancient Egypt typically only live between 28 and 32 years old? The ordinary people primarily ate grain and vegetables, while the kings and leaders indulged in meat. They failed to consume nutritious food, adhere to God's teachings, and maintain proper cooking, hygiene, and sanitation practices. God forbade the consumption of leftover meat due to the absence of refrigeration and methods to preserve it from spoiling. God instructed in his law to observe a waiting period of one week after coming into contact with a deceased being or keeping from a woman during menstruation or after men experience a seminal discharge. Before visiting the purification bath, it was intended to safeguard others from potential contagion through bodily fluids that could lead to illness or death. Interestingly, scientists and doctors discovered many years later that diseases can spread through both blood and genital bodily fluids. We now use washers, dryers, soap, baths, and showers in the place of a purification bath.

Some laws specifically address the presence of black mold in a person's home and on crops. To what extent have scientists and doctors uncovered the harmful impacts of black mold on human health? The laws of God exist to keep us safe from harm. The Holy Spirit in the Garden of Eden protected us from understanding the concept of harm before we were aware of the laws. It is the duty of every man and woman alive to read and uphold the rules, just as the king should. We must also live according to the Holy Spirit and Yeshua, our King, who teaches us his ways and how to live.

Deuteronomy 11:26 says, "Look, today I am giving you a choice between a blessing and a curse!" God does not impose his laws on us, similar to how he didn't do so with Adam and Eve in the garden. God is fair and gives every human freedom to choose how they want to live. The angels also had free will before some decided to sin, and others chose faithfulness to God. We choose to remain in his presence or leave it.

Those who served in the temple during Antiochus' reign over Jerusalem were offered a choice. Some individuals decided to discontinue their involvement in the temple service so they could partake in the gymnasium that Antiochus had built close to the Holy Temple. Many others conformed to society, joining in with the sensual arts, sports, theatre, music, nude exercises, money, prosperity, and sexual immorality. As a result, many had quick surgeries to reverse their circumcisions to look like the rest of society. That reversal symbolized switching one's heart devoted to God and remaining faithful to him. Just as sexual intercourse symbolizes the union between spouses, circumcision of the flesh, particularly that of the heart, represents a profound connection with God. In a marriage, both partners need to be loyal and committed to each other. Similarly, it is important to have faith and commitment toward God, as it is a sign of love.

In Hosea, God compared an unfaithful Israel to an adulterous spouse. However, He promised that if they repent and turn back to obeying his ways, He will heal them of their sins and love them freely. This shows that God's love and forgiveness are always available to those who seek it. God is not an evil, cruel creator that abandons us. On the contrary, He desires to reunite us with Him, so He bestowed us with His commandments and sent us His son to guide us back to holiness.

Prior to Yeshua's arrival, there was a 400-year period of silence with no communication from God. During this time, the people experienced great oppression and suffering. Likewise, slavery persisted in Egypt for a period of 400 years until God intervened in response to the people's immense suffering and oppression by the government. It has also been 400 years since slavery started in America. Although many feel free, are they free from Babylon? How many people are praying to God like Yeshua and Moses did in the past?

May our journey be as righteous as Solomon's, who remained steadfast in his devotion to God from the start. 2 Chronicles 7:1 "As soon as Solomon finished his prayer, fire came down from heaven and consumed the burnt offering and the sacrifices, and the glory of the Lord filled the temple." Let our walk, speech, sacrifices, and prayers be pure before God so that his glory might fill our temple by the fire of his Holy Spirit that consumes the flesh. Let us be humble and pure inside, like the poor widow in Mark 12:43-44 who gave more from her heart than everyone who gave the most from the world. While the disciples were impressed by the grandeur of the temple built by Solomon, Yeshua was amazed by the generosity of a poor widow. The Pharisees and those wealthy in the world failed to recognize her selfless act. Only Yeshua recognized this poor widow who gave her the last coin. Why did God notice this woman? Psalm 24:3-4 "Who may ascend into the hill of the Lord? Or who may stand in His holy place? He who has clean hands and a pure heart, Who has not lifted up his soul to an idol, Nor sworn deceitfully."

I recently observed flowers blooming during spring over a period of days, witnessing their short-lived beauty before they quickly wilted away. While admiring these flowers, I was reminded of Matthew 6:28-30. It struck me how God spoke of the beauty and grandeur of flowers, surpassing even the wealth and splendor of Solomon. Did you catch that? God saw more glory in the flowers, while people saw glory in Solomon. God says in Isaiah 40:7-8 "The grass withers and the flowers fall, because the breath of the Lord blows on them. Surely the people are grass. The grass withers and the flowers fall, but the word of our God endures forever." Everything in this temporary world, including our bodies and the stars, can be fleeting like a fading flower. However, if we live our lives for God and follow His Holy Spirit and teachings, our souls will endure forever in eternity. Not because of our works but because of God's work within us through the cross.

To attain the privilege of standing in the presence of God, we must emulate the examples set forth in the sacred texts. Just as we pondered upon Bethel in the opening of this chapter, we must also embody the spirit of the Samaritan woman from John 4. She was brimming with enthusiasm to receive and spread the good news, eagerly anticipating the arrival of salvation. And let us not forget the pure-hearted Mary, who, in contrast to Martha's preoccupation with worldly affairs and service, humbly sat at the feet of Yeshua, patiently awaiting the arrival of God's eternal deliverance and kingdom. Surrounded by the cloud of his Holy Spirit like Isaiah 4:5, "Then the Lord will provide shade for Mount Zion and all who assemble there. He will provide a canopy of cloud during the day and smoke and flaming fire at night, covering the glorious land."

May you be shaded under his cloud from the world's heat under Adonai and remain on fire in his light through the darkest nights. May you be filled with the smoke of His presence, just as it was in His Temple, until His return. Amen.

CHAPTER 12

Eternity Is Completed

L et's take a trip back to the beginning of this book. Imagine the box, like a coffin, trapping everything inside. But outside the box? That's where eternal life awaits. Think about it. Everything we buy, from the biggest cargo ships to the smallest stores, travels in a box. And it's not just the things we buy that are boxed. Our homes, apartments, and condos are all just boxes. Even the companies we work for are contained within a building, another type of box. Living within the box can limit our perspective. The Pharisees and Sadducees, for example, were so focused on their world that they couldn't see beyond it. They couldn't see the grandeur of Noah's ark or the magnificence of the temple. They were so caught up in their little box that they couldn't fathom eternity. Despite their extensive study of God's word, they could not see beyond the confines of their box. On the other hand, the Spirit can wipe out everything from within, just like Noah's flood. And when that happens, the door to eternity is opened.

Noah's Ark is a true testament to patience and faith in God. It stands solid and unwavering, unaffected by the noise and opinions of the outside world. Constructed by the very word of God, it is a symbol of protection and guidance. In contrast, the temple built by the Sadducees and Pharisees lacked the same unwavering faith. They failed to recognize the word of God before them, blinded by their self-righteousness. The difference between the two is that Noah and his family walked by faith and trusted God's word. They knew the ark was not their final destination but a temporary shelter from the storm. For those who live by faith, the true temple of God is built within. It is not a physical structure but rather a spiritual one that resides in the heart and mind. And while a casket may hold dead bones, the ark within us has the promise of new life and salvation.

In John 9, there is a story of a blind man who was washed in the Pool of Siloam. Yeshua, the Son of God, did something extraordinary. He spat in mud, wiped it on the man's eyes, and then told him to wash in the pool of Siloam. The man trusted by faith and saw eternity before physically seeing with worldly eyes. There's another story that will leave you in wonder. A paralyzed man lay alone by the Pool of Bethesda without help. While everyone else sought their healing at certain times during each day, they would wait anxiously to rush in the water, believing in its healing properties. But the physical healing properties that many sought on Earth were not words written in eternity but within the world's temporary box. The paralyzed man lied there for thirty-eight years with no one to help him, but Yeshua came along and saw the heart and mind of this man. Yeshua said to him, "Do you want to be made well?" the man replied, "Sir, I have no man to put me into the pool when the water is stirred up, but while I am coming, another step down before me." Then Yeshua says, "Rise, take up your bed and walk." How powerful is that? This man trusted God by faith, and God healed him before everyone who rushed to the waters for their healing. Why? This man had faith in the eternal word, "Rise!"

Just as Yeshua commanded Lazarus to rise from the dead, God is urging us to rise up! It's incredible to think that it took thirty-eight years for one man to finally have the faith to look beyond his physical limitations and walk again. There are people out there right now who are waiting for a sign, waiting for the waters to stir, but they don't trust in the power of God's word to lift them up. The word of God has been with us since the beginning, and it has the power to heal us internally and help us endure until the end. Can you imagine being spiritually and physically paralyzed for nearly four decades, all the while hoping and praying for a miraculous healing? The fact that this man was healed and attracted the eyes of Yeshua proves that this paralyzed man saw a greater eternal promise. He wasn't looking for a quick fix or a temporary solution within the box that the flesh desires. Instead, he sought the living waters that flow from above, cleansing both the body and the soul. So let us rise with the power of God's word and the living waters of eternal life and walk boldly with the purpose of God's will and plan!

I consider the significance of the Pool of Siloam and the Pool of Bethsaida; I am hit by their powerful message. The Pool of Siloam, meaning "sent," reminds us of God's ultimate act of love when he sent his son to give sight to the blind. Meanwhile, the Pool of Bethsaida, meaning "house of mercy or grace," speaks to the internal healing the paralyzed received through God's mercy and grace. This story leads me to the next blind man who Jesus healed by the Pool of Bethsaida. Jesus first spit in the mud and put it on the blind man's eyes to restore his sight and asked him, "Do you see anything?" Mark 8:24, he responds, "I see people; they look like trees walking around." This is remarkable because how did he know what trees looked like if he was blind? Perhaps the man heard Micah 4:4, which says, "Each of them will sit under his vine and under his fig tree, with no one to make them afraid, for the mouth of the Lord of hosts has spoken?" After all, maybe God gave him a dream to see the reality of eternity and understand Micah and Jeremiah's prophecy.

In the book of Jeremiah, it's written in chapter 17, verses 7 through 8, "Blessed is the man who trusts in the Lord, And whose hope is the Lord. For he shall be like a tree planted by the waters." This man would have trusted in God sitting beside a peaceful stream, surrounded by lush trees, meditating on the words of eternity until the Messiah returns for him. And just like this man, if you continue to endure and trust in God, He will return for you too. The blind man would have heard in the synagogues the words of Isaiah 29:18 "In that day the deaf shall hear the words of a book, and out of their gloom and darkness the eyes of the blind shall see." Isaiah also states in 32:3, "Then the eyes of those who see will not be closed, and the ears of those who hear will give attention." The blind man received the word not in the temporary but in the eternal. Look even further into the words in Mark 8:25-26 "Once more Jesus put his hands on the man's eyes. Then his eyes were opened, his sight was restored, and he saw everything clearly. Jesus sent him home, saying, "Don't even go into the village."

Upon being touched for the first time, the blind man said, "I see people like trees walking around." After being touched by Yeshua once more, he saw clearly. This demonstrates that God can grant us the ability to see through His eyes. This man's faith in Jesus allowed him to see the world in a whole new light. We may not always see life clearly, but when we grow in faith and understanding, we can begin to comprehend the wonders that God has shown us. This blind man heard the word of God and received it with faith, allowing him to see and understand the world around him. Romans 10:17 says, "Faith comes by hearing, and hearing by the word of God." By having faith in Yeshua and the word of God, we can gain the ability to see and hear and to walk in his ways. Like the deaf man in Mark 7:31-37 who also had a speech impediment, Yeshua once again put his finger in his ears, spit in his hand, touched his tongue, then the man spoke and heard. How did this man who couldn't hear or hardly speak receive healing from God?

God has a way of choosing those who may not seem like the obvious choice to the world. Just like the Pool of Siloam, God selects individuals who may not be viewed as ideal in the eyes of society. Take Moses, for example. He was not eloquent, nor was he quick-witted. In fact, he was slow in speech and tongue. But God saw something in him that others did not. He saw his humility, his introverted nature, and his willingness to follow God's plan. Exodus 4:10-11 "Moses said to the Lord, "Oh, my Lord, I am not eloquent, either in the past or since you have spoken to your servant, but I am slow of speech and of tongue." Then the Lord said to him, "Who has made man's mouth? Who makes him mute, or deaf, or seeing, or blind? Is it, not I, the Lord?" And so, God chose Moses, who spent 40 years alone in the wilderness, to lead his people out of Egypt.

God sees what is inside of a man rather than what is outside. God sees beyond what is on the surface. He looks at the heart of a person rather than their outward appearance. Just like when He told Samuel not to judge by worldly standards but to look at what was inside a person. 1 Samuel 16:7, "The Lord said to Samuel, "Do not consider his appearance or his height, for I have rejected him. The Lord does not look at the things people look at. People look at the outward appearance, but the Lord looks at the heart." He's not interested in those obsessed with this world's fleeting pleasures. Instead, he's searching for those who have an eternal perspective and are willing to let him reside in their souls. It's like comparing a beautiful, vibrant garden to a dull, white-washed tomb. Which would you rather be?

In John 9:2-3, the disciples of Yeshua asked him, "Rabbi, who sinned, this man or his parents, that he was born blind?" "Neither this man nor his parents sinned," said Yeshua, "but this happened so that the works of God might be displayed in him." It's easy to fall into the trap of assuming that those who are sick or disabled must have done something wrong to deserve their afflictions. His disciples believed this man sinned. But Yeshua saw the healing that needed to occur not just in the body but also in the soul. However, the Pharisees and Sadducees were blind to this truth. They were more focused on outward appearances and following the letter of the law that they couldn't see the miracles happening right before them. As Matthew 23:25 reveals, "Woe to you, teachers of the law and Pharisees, you hypocrites! You clean the outside of the cup and dish, but inside, they are full of greed and self-indulgence." The Torah Teachers and Pharisees were visually appealing on the outside, just like the temple was beautiful to the eye. But on the inside, they were corrupt and decayed, white-washed tombs full of dead bones, as Yeshua states. They couldn't fathom eternity or how the blind, sick, and lame were being healed by the power of God and seeing eternity. Yeshua attempted to guide them in his infinite mercy and grace, but they were unwilling to receive the one sent from above. As a result, they remained trapped in a state of spiritual blindness, physical lameness, deafness, paralysis, and sickness both in this life and for all eternity.

I think about the message of Shavuot, also known as Pentecost. God gave Moses his laws on Mount Sinai, and on the same day, Yeshua filled 5000 people in Acts 4 with his Holy Spirit. The laws of God are no longer just written on tablets of stone but within the hearts and minds of those who believe. God says in Isaiah 26:3, "You will keep him in perfect peace, whose mind is stayed on You Because he trusts in You." This is the message of Pentecost and Shavuot. When we keep God at the forefront of our minds, we can experience perfect peace. We may see the chaos and uncertainty of the world around us, but we can trust God's plan when we focus on eternity. Don't let the devil convince you that you're not a child of the living God. You have a purpose, and it's by God's grace and mercy that you're here. He's sending you out to bring him glory, all while remaining at peace.

There's a reason he told his disciples in Matthew 10:13, "If the household is worthy, let your peace come upon it. But if it's not worthy, let your peace return to you." God wants you to remain in his peace and love, no matter what the world throws your way. He promises, "I will never leave you nor forsake you." As Psalm 32:8 says, "I will instruct you and teach you in the way you should go; I will counsel you with my eye upon you." We must remember 1 Peter 3:12, "For the eyes of the Lord are on the righteous, and his ears are open to their prayer. But the face of the Lord is against those who do evil." So let's strive to do good and avoid evil because the face of the Lord is against those who do wrong.

You are the temple of God. Throughout history, whenever the temple stood, if the priests were sinning and living in it, the presence and Spirit of God departed. But those born in Yeshua are made clean! However, you must rest with God like Samuel sleeping in his temple, waiting for his gentle voice. God wants to keep his Spirit close to you, with your ears open and your mouth speaking to him often. As the word says, "pray without ceasing," and the Shema written in Deuteronomy, 6:3-9 repeats to think about his statutes and ordinances constantly and to "Love Adonai your God with all your heart, and with all your soul, and with all your strength." In doing so, we will have a heart full of love, a soul full of peace, and strength greater than Sampson. Keep your purity with Adonai, and do not let the world take your strength as Delilah did with Sampson. Let your strength become whole like Sampson killing 3000 enemies with a donkey's jawbone. Let your strength be found in Yeshua, slaying the demons in your life by the word of God and through the power of His Spirit. Like David, who walked by faith and wiped out the giant in his life with a stone, let that stone that Yeshua was removed from your heart become used to take out the giant in your own life, causing the enemies of demons to flee. Like David, who laid down the weapons and armor given by man, let your armor and strength be in God, his word, and the weapons within which he has given you. Keep your ears open, your mouth speaking to God often, and your heart full of love. You are the temple of God, and He wants to keep his Spirit close to you.

Sling that stone at the giant in your life, and let your faith be made whole in the one who gives you strength like David fighting the lion to protect the lambs. Let's be humble, like David, not taking pride in the kingdom on Earth, like his son Absalom, who was greedy for the temporary kingdom. David would have given Absalom the entire kingdom, yet his appetite for more in the world brought him bitter death.

Let's not be like Jeroboam, who had temporary eyes for pleasure, greed, power, and satisfying his worldly desires. He formed his idols and set up his method of worship for the people. Let's not be like Rehoboam, who did not care for the well-being of his neighbors while increasing heavy taxes and working on others. Let's follow in the footsteps of Hananiah, Mishael, and Azariah, who refused to bow down to worship the idols and false religions of the worldly kingdom. They remained steadfast in their faith, even to the point of death, rather than compromise their belief. God saved them without a scorch on their heads despite being thrown into the flames. They saw the eternity of heaven over the eternity of the flames. They realized that life on Earth was transitory, regardless of whether God saved them or not. They also understood that following the world's idols and worship could not live on in the kingdom to come.

Let's be like Caleb. Fearless in the face of the giants! While other believers cowered in fear, Caleb and Joshua stood firm in their faith, trusting God's promise of a land and a kingdom. They refused to complain or doubt, and as a result, they could enter into God's rest and peace. The others with them grumbled and lacked the faith to trust in God's word and promise, and as a result, they were unable to enter into his rest. Hebrews 3:11 says, "I swore in My wrath, 'They shall not enter My rest.'" They did not enter the rest and peace of God because they were not willing to walk by faith and trust in his word and promise. Remember Isaiah 26:3? He will keep in perfect peace whose mind's set on Him! You will remain in His rest if you keep your heart, soul, and mind on Him. So let's be like Caleb and Joshua and trust in God's promises with unwavering faith!

Hebrews 3:12 encourages us to be vigilant and not let sin or temptation overpower our walk with God. "See to it, brothers and sisters, that none of you has a sinful, unbelieving heart that turns away from the living God." Be careful to walk with God. We must strive to be like Joshua, Caleb, and Moses, who God recognized for their faith, while over a million people lacked faith. Even those who witnessed the signs and miracles of God in Egypt did not believe. As it's written in Hebrews 3:18-19 "To whom did He swear that they would not enter His rest? Was it not to those who were disobedient? So we see that they were not able to enter in because of lack of trust." Let our trust remain steadfast, not living in disobedience and sin. Let's strive to be like Elisha, who left his plow, burnt the mantle, and fed everyone the cooked oxen from his job upon seeing the arrival of Elijah. Elisha saw living and laboring for the glory of God and obedience to Him as the most fulfilling and rewarding part of his life. Let us also be filled with that same desire and perspective as we look beyond this temporary life and gaze past the universe into eternity within our souls and outside of the depthless infinite realm of the universe.

May eternity become the most captivating fulfillment of our senses as the world and the things in it begin to fade away. Let us be like Hannah, who cried out to God for a child so that she could dedicate him to God and serve Him. As a result, a faithful son named Samuel grew up to live faithfully to God until the end. Likewise, Let us desire to raise our children as faithful sons and daughters for service and devotion to God. We must be careful not to become treacherous and violent like Joab, who killed innocent men despite being a strong fighter for David. We should be cautious not to let our strength and power go to our heads, causing harm to others and becoming a threat to their spiritual well-being. We should rather live to encourage each other as it's written in 1

Thessalonians 5:11, "Therefore encourage one another and build each other up."

We must also be mindful of Jonah's life. He resisted God's calling and ended up in the belly of a whale until he repented and agreed to follow God's will. The belly of the whale represents the depths within our being that wars against God, resisting his peace and obedience. It's a place where our will becomes swallowed up and then submits to the will of God. We know that he was low and depressed and willing to walk himself off the ship to his death. God had other plans to bring glory to His name. We must submit to the will of God and not run from Him.

One who wrestles or runs from God will never have peace inside like Jacob wrestling with God, who experienced a permanent limp. God will drown you inside until you give up, repent, and yield to his obedience, love, grace, and peace again. As God speaks in Isaiah 43:2, "When you pass through the waters, I will be with you; And through the rivers, they will not overflow you. When you walk through the fire, you will not be scorched, Nor will the flame burn you." God declares that nothing will harm us in this life, and he will be with us. Think about Hananiah, Mishael, and Azariah. Think about Joshua and Moses walking through the Red Sea and the Jordan River; the waters did not touch them. In the same way, if we keep our minds focused on God, like Isaiah 26:3, we will not be affected by the storms of life.

Let us be like Gideon, who saw the miracles of God in his life. As a result, he acted upon his faith and won great battles in life. It's important to stay vigilant and not lose faith, as well as avoid falling into the same traps as Gideon did later on. He struggled with pride, guilt, and idolatry, which took root within him. Let's complete this race with determination until the very end, all while remembering God's incredible miracles in our lives. It's interesting how we can easily recall a thousand good deeds someone has done for us and cherish them, but as soon as they say or do something hurtful, we tend to forget all the good and solely focus on the one negative action. Sadly, many can live their life like this with God. It's essential to reflect on the incredible things God has done in the past, but during difficult times, we may tend to dwell on the hardships of life. This can cause us to overlook how God has delivered us in the past and instead become overly fixated on our present negative trials and situations. It's important to hold onto these memories as we progress toward peace.

Becoming someone after God's own heart requires testing and walking through the wilderness of your inner soul. As Yeshua says in Mark 7:20-23 "It is what comes out of the man that makes the man unholy. From within, out of the heart of men, come evil intentions, sexual immorality, theft, murder, adultery, greed, wickedness, deceit, lustfulness, envy, slander, pride, and foolishness. All these evil things come from within and make the man unholy."

Take David, for example. David was tested with pride, murder, lust, and adultery. These things defiled him, yet his heart of repentance and turning from these actions revealed he had a heart after God's. Read into the writings of Psalms. A heart like that spent much time with God in deep anguish, joy, love, forgiveness, hope, pain, suffering, kindness, peace, and self-control. David demonstrated his sincere remorse for his past indulgence in lust, as evidenced by his behavior towards a beautiful young woman brought to him by his servants towards the end of his life. Despite being presented with a tempting opportunity by his servants in the form of a stunning young woman, David exercised admirable self-restraint. He refrained from engaging in any inappropriate behavior. His upright conduct was a testament to his personal growth and development of self-control and his genuine concern for the well-being of those around him. David was not perfect, but he had a heart of repentance and desired to walk and live for God. We must also have a heart after God's own heart and be filled with the fruits of the Spirit. We must trust in the Lord with all our hearts, not lean on our own understanding, and have the humility to change and do what is right.

God may allow tests to arise again in the future to determine if we've truly learned from the past. While we may succeed in some tests, we may also encounter some that we don't pass. But the heart after God cries out Psalm 86:11, "Teach me your way, Adonai, that I may rely on your faithfulness; give me an undivided heart, that I may fear your name." As the writings of Psalm 119 cries from within one's soul, and verse 47 speaks, "I will delight in your commandments because I love them." Proverbs 21:2 says, "Every way of a man is right in his own eyes, but the Lord weighs the heart." Let God check your heart while waiting with patience and humility for him to reveal it to you.

Proverbs 3:5. "Trust in the Lord with all your heart, and do not lean on your own understanding." May we trust God in everything we do, feel, think, and do. Let our entire being trust in him, not ourselves or the creation around us that we can see and touch. If Yeshua says, "I leave you my peace." that is his gift to us in this body and on this Earth in this physical dimension. We can often search for anything in the world to bring us peace, but without the love of God and believing in his son Yeshua, there will never be peace in the universe or within ourselves. You might find temporary relief like a massage, warm shower or bath, exercise, stretching, traveling, or resting on the beach or mountain, but there will still be a stirring inside your soul. Like the waters of Bethsaida seeking healing and rest, one must seek out the living waters that flow beyond this dimension to heal the soul.

This discovery comes from Yeshua and his faith, while rest and peace come from true repentance. If we want eternity to become a reality in our lives more and more every day, we must find contentment with resting in God's holy words, like sleeping on the Bible and covering up with his pages within our souls. We will have the rest and comfort of His embrace, knowing that no man can pluck you out of His hand. The choice is yours to rest and lay beside still waters or live a life of raging seas. Do you want to discover the secret of how Yeshua could sleep peacefully during the storm on the boat? Or find yourself feeling restless and fearful when faced with similar circumstances?

Contentment says, "I have found peace. What more could I want?" It also says, "The still waters are all I love. I have nothing else to gain." The one who has discovered eternity knows that God brings peace and contentment. The question within your soul and the universe remains up to one's discovery. What do you see? Do you view the world as Yeshua ascending into heaven or as Yeshua being dead? What about seeing him descending and returning like Jacobs's ladder with the angels and Spirit going up and down? Do you see the waterfall flowing from the temple beyond the universe in heaven and into one's soul? Can you feel his saving grace and his presence all around you? Has one found contentment in knowing this body is perishing, but the soul is living for eternity right now?

The things we perceive may only be illusions, but the actuality exists beyond this realm. It's important to have faith in the teachings of God and the redemptive power of Yeshua. The more we grasp eternity, the more peace and contentment we can receive. The closer we reach heaven's gates, the more prayer, contentment, and rest can fill us inside. As David says in Psalm 23:1-3 "Adonai is my shepherd, I shall not want. He makes me lie down in green pastures. He leads me beside still waters. He restores my soul. He guides me in paths of righteousness for His Name's sake."

As Solomon wrote in Ecclesiastes 3:11, "He has made everything beautiful in its time. He has also set eternity in the human heart, yet no one can fathom what God has done from beginning to end." As Yeshua says in John 5:24, "Very truly I tell you, whoever hears my word and believes him who sent me has eternal life and will not be judged but has crossed over from death to life." Also, in John 17:3-4 "And this is eternal life, that they may know You, the only true God, and Yeshua the Messiah, the One You sent."

His words are the key to eternal life from Genesis to Revelation. Matthew 6:21 says, "For where your treasure is, there your heart will also be." One should go back to the parable of the pearl and ask where their treasure is. The universe has real physical gems, even on the scientific table of elements. Still, the treasure from beyond the universe can only be discovered from within by faith in Yeshua and hearing God's word. The Pharisees had the treasures of the world's possessions and the written word, yet failed to uncover the treasure that lies beyond the universe through faith.

The question still remains: Is the precious treasure in my heart, soul, and mind? Or does it still exist in the tangible universe we observe? Is it in the unseen realm of heaven?

In Matthew 2:11, the wise men brought Yeshua their treasure after his birth. Later, Mary poured her expensive perfume on Yeshua's feet, and then the rich man gave Yeshua his tomb to be buried. Do you think their hearts and treasures were in eternity? Even more, God is looking for those with characteristics in Matthew 5 and those he can fill with the fruits of the Spirit. He seeks those with faith as small as a mustard seed in an endless universe where he can water and grow for his kingdom. The mind sustained upon God is like Adam and Eve with the Spirit of God before they were preoccupied with guilt, shame, and sin.

Allow Yeshua to renew your mind and life, enabling you to have a mind focused on eternity and nourished by the Spirit within, just like the garden in the New Jerusalem. Luke 17:20-21 says, "The coming of the kingdom of God is not something that can be observed, nor will people say, 'Here it is,' or 'There it is,' because the kingdom of God is in your midst (within you)."

Live your lives by faith for eternity! Amen!

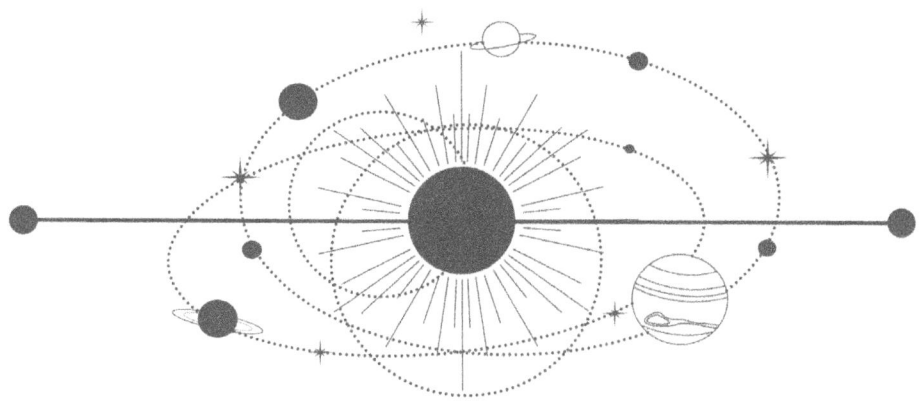

"The early church was married to poverty, prisons, and persecutions. Today, the church is married to prosperity, personality, and popularity."

"5 minutes into eternity, and we will wish that we had sacrificed more, wept more, loved more, grieved more, prayed more, sweated more, and given more."

"We are not eternity conscious enough."
"At any point in all of Eternity, we can say, "This is just the beginning." How wonderful for those who are with Christ. How unimaginably dreadful for those who are not."

"This life is a dressing room for eternity, that's all it is!"
-Leonard Ravenhill